LOOKING AT PHILOSOPHY
The Unbearable Heaviness of Philosophy Made Lighter
Second Edition

Text and Illustrations
by

DONALD PALMER

LOOKING AT PHILOSOPHY
The Unbearable Heaviness of Philosophy Made Lighter

Second Edition

DONALD PALMER
College of Marin

Mayfield Publishing Company
Mountain View, California
London • Toronto

Library of Congress Cataloging-in-Publication Data

Palmer, Donald.
    Looking at Philosophy : the unbearable heaviness of philosophy
  made lighter / Donald Palmer.—2nd ed.
        p.   cm.
  Includes bibliographical references and index.
  ISBN 1–55934–230-7
    1. Philosophy—History. 2. Philosophy—History—Caricatures and
  cartoons. 3. American wit and humor, Pictorial. I. Title.
  B74 . P26 1993
  190—dc20

                                 93–4006
                                     CIP

Manufactured in the United States of America

15   14   13

Mayfield Publishing Company
1280 Villa Street
Mountain View, CA 94041

Sponsoring editor, James Bull; production editor, Sondra Glider;
manuscript editor, Betty Duncan; text and cover designer, Robin
Mouat; manufacturing manager, Martha Branch. Illustrations by
Donald Palmer. The text was set in 13/18 Tekton and printed on
50# Text White Opaque by Maple-Vail Book Manufacturing
Group.

CONTENTS

PREFACE

Wittgenstein once said that a whole philosophy book could be written consisting of nothing but jokes. THIS IS NOT THAT BOOK, nor does this book treat the history of philosophy as a joke. This book takes philosophy seriously, but not gravely. As the subtitle indicates, the goal of the book is to lighten the load a bit. How to do this without simply throwing the cargo overboard? First, by presenting an overview of Western philosophy from the sixth century B.C. through three-quarters of the twentieth century in a way that introduces the central philosophical ideas of the West and their evolution in a concise, readable format without trivializing them, but at the same time, without pretending to have exhausted them nor to have plumbed their depths. Second, following a time-honored medieval tradition, by illuminating the margins of the text. Some of these illuminations, namely, those that attempt to schematize difficult ideas, I hope will be literally illuminating. Most of them, however, are simply attempts in a lighter vein to interrupt the natural propensity of the philosophers to succumb to the pull of gravity. (Nietzsche said that only the grave lay in that direction.) But even these philosophical jokes, I hope, have a pedagogical function. They should serve to help the reader retain the ideas that are thereby gently mocked. Twenty years of teaching the subject, which I love—and which has provoked more than a few laughs on the part of my students—convinces me that this technique should work. I do not claim to have achieved Nietzsche's "Joyful wisdom," but I agree with him that there is such a thing and that we should strive for it.

Before turning you over to Thales and his metaphysical water (the first truly heavy water), I want to say a word about the women and their absence. Why are there so few women in a book of this nature? There are a number of possible explanations, including these:

1. Women really are deficient in the capacity for sublimation, hence are incapable of participating in higher culture (as Schopenhauer and Freud suggested).

2. Women have in fact contributed greatly to the history of philosophy, but their contributions have been denied or suppressed by the chauvinistic male writers of the histories of philosophy.

3. Women have been (intentionally or unintentionally) systematically eliminated from the history of philosophy by political, social, religious, and psychological manipulations of power by a deeply entrenched, jealous, and fearful patriarchy.

I am certain that the first thesis does not merit our serious attention. I think there is some truth to the second thesis, and I may be partially guilty of suppressing that truth. For example, the names of at least seventy women philosophers in the late classical period alone have been recorded, foremost of which are Aspasia, Diotima, Aretê, and Hypatia. (Hypatia has been belatedly honored by having a journal of feminist philosophy recently named after her.) Jumping over centuries to our own age, we find a number of well-known women contributing to the history of philosophy in the first half of the current century, including Simone de Beauvoir, Susanne Langer, and L. Susan Stebbing.

However, no matter how original, deep, and thought-provoking were the ideas of these philosophers, I believe that, for a number of reasons (those reasons given in the second and third theses are probably most pertinent here), none of them has been as historically significant as those philosophers who have been dealt with in this book. Fortunately, things have begun to change in the last few years. An adequate account of contemporary philosophy could not in good faith ignore the major contributions to the analytic tradition of philosophers like Iris Murdoch, Philippa Foot, G. E. M. Anscombe, and Judith Jarvis Thompson, nor those contributions to the continental tradition made by Gayatri Chakravorty Spivak, Monique Wittig, Luce Irigaray, and Julia Kristeva. Furthermore, a new wave of feminist philosophers is already beginning to have considerable impact on the content of contemporary philosophy and not merely on its style.

So, despite the risks, I defend the third thesis. I truly believe that if women had not been systematically excluded from major participation in the history of philosophy, that history would be even richer, deeper, more compassionate, and more interesting (not to mention more joyful) than it already is. It is not for nothing that the book ends with a discussion of the work of a contemporary feminist philosopher and with a question posed to philosophy herself, "Quo vadis?"—Whither goest thou?

The second edition of this book has involved numerous transformations. Several sections have been rewritten and there have been some corrections and several expansions. Additions include new segments on John Dewey and Martin Heidegger, and the book is brought more up to date by moving ahead from the 1950s to the 1970s. Also a short annotated bibliography has been added.

Finally, I want to say that I have had some help with both editions of this book. For assistance with the first edition I am grateful to Kerry Walk and reviewers Job Clement, Daytona Beach Community College; Hans Hansen, Wayne State University; Yukio Shirahama, San Antonio College; and William Tinsley, Foothill College, who read parts of the manuscript and provided helpful suggestions. Donald Porter, College of San Mateo, read the whole thing. He clearly understood exactly what I was trying to achieve and gave me many good ideas for doing it better. For help with the second edition, I am indebted to Dasiea Cavers-Huff, Riverside Community College; Donald Porter, College of San Mateo; Matt Schulte, Montgomery College; and Robert White, Mongomery College. Jim Bull, my editor at Mayfield Publishing Company, had faith in this project from its inception. He has provided unqualified support from its halting start to the completion of the second edition. My thanks to Sondra Glider and Robin Mouat of Mayfield's Production Department for their expertise. My wife Leila May has been my most acute critic and my greatest source of inspiration. She kept me laughing during the dreariest stages of the production of the manuscript, often finding on its pages jokes that weren't meant to be there. I hope she managed to catch most of them. There probably are still a few pages that are funnier than I intended them to be.

《 》

For Katarina & Christian

LOOKING AT PHILOSOPHY

INTRODUCTION

The story of Western philosophy begins in

GREECE

The Greek word LOGOS designates a certain kind of thinking about the world, a kind of logical analysis that places things in the context of reason and explains them with the pure force of thought. Such an intellectual exercise was supposed to lead to wisdom (<u>Sophia</u>), and those who dedicated themselves to Logos were thought of as lovers of wisdom (love = <u>philo</u>), hence as <u>philosophers</u>.

What was there before philosophy, before Logos? There was <u>mythos</u>—a certain way of thinking that placed the world in the context of its supernatural origins. Mythos explained worldly things by tracing them to exceptional, sometimes sacred, events that caused the world to be as it is now. In the case of the Greeks, this meant tracing them to the dramatic acts of the gods of Mount Olympus. The narratives describing these origins—myths— are not only explanatory but also morally exemplary and ritualistically instructive. Hence, they are often conservative in nature. They seek to maintain the status quo by replicating origins: "So behaved the sacred ancestors, so must we behave." Myths had the advantage

Explaining Ancient Greek Customs

2

of creating a whole social world in which all acts had meaning. They had the disadvantage of creating static societies, of resisting innovation, and, many would say, of being false. Then, suddenly, philosophy happened—Logos broke upon the scene, at least, according to the traditional account. (There <u>are</u> other accounts, however, accounts that suggest that Western Logos—philosophy and science—is just <u>our</u> version of myth.) But let us suppose that something different <u>did</u> take place in Greece about 700 B.C. Let's suppose that the "first" philosopher's explanation of the flooding of the Nile River during the summer (most rivers tend to dry up in the summer) as being caused by desert winds (<u>desert</u> <u>winds</u>, NOT battles or love affairs among gods) really does constitute novelty. Natural phenomena are explained by other natural phenomena, not by supernatural events in "dream time." In that case, Greece truly is the cradle of Western philosophy.

A Modern Myth?

Why Greece, and not, for example, Egypt or Judea?
Well, for one reason, there was no PRIESTLY CLASS of
CENSORS in Greece.

For another, the Greek imagination had always been fer-
tile, and concerned with intimate detail. For example, Homer's
description of Achilles' shield takes up four pages of the Iliad.

Furthermore, the Greeks were particularly aware of CHANGE, of the war of the opposites, summer to winter, hot to cold, light to dark, and that most dramatic change of all, life to death.

Indeed, this sensitivity to the transitory nature of all things sometimes led the Greeks to PESSIMISM. (The poet Simonides wrote, "Generations of men fall like the leaves of the forest.")

But it also led them to demand an
EXPLANATION—

one that would be obtained and justified not by the authority of religious tradition but by the sheer power of human reason. Here we find an optimism behind the pessimism—the human mind operating on its own devices is able to discover ultimate truths about reality.

I.
THE PRE-SOCRATIC
PHILOSOPHERS

The first dispassionate attempt at such an explanation
was carried out by THALES of MILETUS (ca. 580 B.C.), who
was the first to be recorded as a true philosopher.

If there is change, there must be some THING that changes, yet does not change. There must be a unity behind the apparent plurality of things, a Oneness disguised by the superficial plurality of the world.

Like the myth makers before him, Thales was familiar with the four elements: AIR, FIRE, WATER, and EARTH. He assumed that all things must ultimately be reducible to

one of these four—BUT WHICH ONE?

Of all the elements, water is the most obvious in its transformations: Rivers turn into deltas, water turns into ice, then back into water, which in turn can be changed into steam, which becomes air, and air, in the form of wind, fans fire.

Then water it is!
ALL THINGS ARE COMPOSED OF WATER.

This obviously false conclusion is valued today not for its CONTENT but for its FORM (. . . it is not a great leap between the claim "All things are composed of water" and the claim "All things are composed of atoms") and for the presupposition behind it (. . . that there is an ultimate stuff behind appearances that explains change while remaining itself unchanged).

Still, not all of Thales' contemporaries accepted his formulation. ANAXIMANDER (ca. 610–ca. 546 B.C.), for one, said, "If all things were water, then long ago everything would have returned to water." He asked how water could become its deadly enemy, fire—how a quality could give rise to its opposite.

No, for Anaximander, the ultimate stuff behind the four elements could not itself be one of the elements. It would have to be an unobservable, unspecific, indeterminate something-or-other, which he called "the Boundless," or "the Unlimited." It would <u>have</u> to be "boundless," "unlimited," and "unspecific" because anything *specific* is opposed to all the other specific things in existence. (Water is not fire, which in turn is *not* air, . . .) Yet the Boundless is opposed to nothing, because everything is IT.

Anaximander seems to have imagined the Boundless as originally moving effortlessly in a great cosmic vortex, which was interrupted by some disaster

(a Big Bang?), which caused the four elements to "separate off" from the vortex. In one of the few passages remaining to us from the book he wrote, Anaximander says:

And from what source things arise, to that they return of necessity when they are destroyed, for they suffer punishment and make reparation to one another for their injustice according to the order of time.

There are many possible interpretations of this amazing passage. According to the most dramatic interpretation, the whole world as you and I know it is the result of a cosmic error. Creation is an act of injustice. But justice will be done; the world will eventually be destroyed, and "things" will return to their boundless source and revolve eternally in a vortex. <u>This</u> interpretation, which contains at least as much Mythos as Logos, exhibits a bizarre kind of optimism about the triumph of Justice.

A less radical and less mythical interpretation would be this: Once the four elements were created, they became related to one another in antagonistic ways, but their opposition to one another balances out in an ecological harmony. If one element dominates at one period (say, water in a time of flood), it will later be compensated by the domination of another element at another period (say, fire in a drought). So the original unity of the Boundless is preserved in the apparent war of the opposites.

Some of Anaximander's followers asked, "How much better is an 'unspecific, indeterminate something-or-other' than nothing at all?" They decided that it was NO better, in fact, it was the SAME as nothing at all, and, knowing that EX NIHILO NIHIL (from nothing comes nothing), they went on searching for the mysterious ultimate stuff.

The next philosopher,
ANAXIMENES (ca. 545 B.C.), thought it was AIR.

The air that we experience ("commonsense" air) is a halfway house between all the other forms into which "primordial air" can be transformed through CONDENSATION and RAREFACTION.

Rarefaction

fire
smoke
steam
AIR
mist
water
mud
dirt
stone

Condensation

With the idea of condensation and rarefaction, Anaximenes introduced the important claim that all differences in quality are really differences in quantity (just more or less STUFF packed into a specific space), an idea with which many scientists would agree today.

These first three philosophers, Thales, Anaximander, and Anaximenes, are known as the MILESIANS because they all came from the Greek colony of Miletus on the Persian coast and because they constitute the first <u>school</u> of philosophy. Despite the differences among them, they shared a number of characteristics, some of which would eventually become part of the Western scientific tradition—a desire for simple explanations, a reliance on observation to support their theories, a commitment to **naturalism** (the view that natural phenomena should be explained in terms of other natural phenomena), and **monism** (the view that ultimately there is only one kind of "stuff").

The School of Miletus ended when the tenuous peace between the Greek outpost and Persia collapsed and the Persians overran the city.

The Milesians' successor, PYTHAGORAS (ca. 572–ca. 500 B.C.), did not seek ultimacy in some material element, as his predecessors had done. Rather, he held the curious view that all things are numbers. Literally understood, this seems absurd, but among other things, Pythagoras meant that a correct description of reality must be expressed in terms of mathematical formulas.

Furthermore, he anticipated the bulk of Euclid's writings on geometry and discovered the ratios of concord between musical sound and number. From this he deduced a mathematical harmony throughout the universe, a view that led to the doctrine of "the Music of the Spheres."

The influence of Pythagoras was so great that the School of Pythagoreans lasted almost 400 years. The spell he cast on Plato alone would be enough to guarantee Pythagoras a permanent place in the history of philosophy.

There was another, less scientific aspect of Pythagoras's teachings, which should be noted. He was the leader of a religious cult whose members had to obey a strict number of esoteric rules based on asceticism, numerology, and vegetarianism.

Despite their vegetarianism, Pythagoreans had to forswear eating beans because eating beans is a form of cannibalism. A close look at the inside of a bean reveals that each one contains a small, embryonic human being (or human bean, as the case may be).

The next philosopher, HERACLITUS (ca. 470 B.C.), had a new insight:

The basic stuff is FIRE!

though he seems to have understood this idea more in a metaphorical than in a literal sense.

There is something about the nature of fire that explains both the appearance of STABILITY (the flame's FORM is stable) . . . and the FACT of CHANGE (in the flame, everything changes). Heraclitus drew some striking conclusions from this insight.

Reality is composed not of a number of THINGS but
of a PROCESS of continual creation and destruction.
"War Is King."

"You can't step in the same river twice."
"Everything changes but change itself."

Heraclitus was called "the Dark One." His ideas were interpreted pessimistically. They create more than merely a philosophy—they constitute a MOOD, almost a worldview of nostalgia and loss.

You can't go home again. Your childhood is lost.
The friends of your youth are gone.
Your present is slipping away from you.
Nothing is ever the same.

Nevertheless, there was something positive in the Heraclitian philosophy. There existed an unobservable Logos—a logic—governing change that made change a rational phenomenon rather than the chaotic, arbitrary one it appeared to be. This Logos doctrine deeply impressed Plato and eventually became the basis of the notion of natural law.

Heraclitus's successor PARMENIDES (ca. 515–ca. 440 B.C.) went a step further than his predecessor.

In effect, he said that you can't step in the same river ONCE.

Parmenides begins with what he takes to be a self-evident truth: IT IS. This is not an empirical claim—not one derived from observation—rather it is a truth of Reason. It cannot even be denied without self-contradiction. If you say, "IT IS NOT" (i.e., nothing exists), then you've proved that "IT IS"; for if nothing exists, it's not nothing, rather it is something.

Parmenides believes that Being is rational, that only what can be thought can exist. Since "Nothing" cannot be thought (without thinking of it as something), there is no nothing, there is only Being. From the mere idea of Being it follows that Being is uncreated, indestructible, eternal, indivisible, and equally real in all directions. Being has no holes (no vacuum) because, if Being IS, there can't be any place where Being is NOT.

From this it follows that motion is impossible because motion would involve Being going from where Being is to where being isn't (but there can't BE any such place as the place where Being isn't).

In a series of famous paradoxes, Parmenides' disciple, the sly old fox ZENO of Elea (ca. 490 B.C.–?), "proved" the impossibility of motion using a method known as *reductio ad absurdum*.

In this form of argument, you begin by accepting your opponent's premises, and you demonstrate that they lead logically to an absurdity or a contradiction.

Zeno argued that, even granting motion, one could never arrive anywhere, not even to such a simple goal as a door. Before you can get to the door, you must go halfway, but before you can go halfway, you must go halfway of the remaining halfway, but before you can do that, you must go halfway of halfway, but before you can go halfway, you must go halfway. When does this argument end? Never! It goes on to infinity. Therefore, motion would be impossible even if it were possible.

In yet another of his paradoxes, Zeno demonstrated that in a race between Achilles and a tortoise, if Achilles gave the tortoise a head start (as would only be fair), the swift runner could never overtake the lumbering reptile. This is because, before Achilles can pass the tortoise, he must arrive at the point where the tortoise used to be; but given the hypothesis of motion, the tortoise will never still be there. He will have moved on. This will forever be the case. When Achilles arrives at a point where the tortoise was, the tortoise will have progressed. Achilles can never catch him.

Parmenides and Zeno caused a crisis in Greek philosophy. First, they forced the distinction between information based on the five senses and that based on pure reason (a distinction that will later develop into two schools of philosophy: **empiricism** and **rationalism**); second, they forced a reevaluation of the monistic presupposition accepted by all Greeks heretofore (namely, the view that reality is composed of ONE THING) because thinkers came to realize that such a view led directly to Parmenides' untenable conclusions.

Is Reality One Thing?

Or Many?

The next group of philosophers are known as PLURAL-ISTS, precisely because they believed that ultimate reality is composed of a plurality of things rather than of only one kind of thing.

The first of this group was EMPEDOCLES (?–ca. 440 B.C.), who believed that everything was composed of the simplest parts of the four elements: fire, air, earth, and water. He called these elements the "four roots."

But in the face of Zeno's critique of motion, Empedocles believed he needed to posit two forces to explain change and movement. These he called LOVE and STRIFE. Love is the force of unity, bringing together unrelated items to produce new creations, and strife is the force of destruction, breaking down old unities into fragments.

(Empedocles' theory was later to be accepted by Freud, who named the two forces EROS and THANATOS [the life instinct and the death instinct]. Freud agreed with Empedocles that these forces formed the bases of all organic matter.)

The first theory of evolution developed out of Empedocles' system. Love brings together certain kinds of monsters. ". . . many heads grew up without necks, and arms were wandering about naked, bereft of shoulders, and eyes roamed about alone with no foreheads."

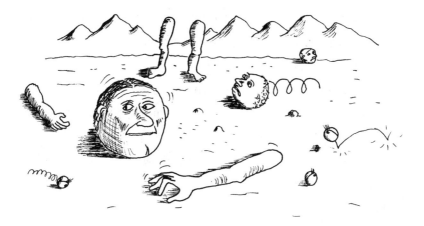

And those that could survive, did survive. (Aristotle later criticized this view as "leaving too much to chance.")

The next pluralist, ANAXAGORAS (ca. 500–ca. 428 B.C.), found Empedocles' theory too simplistic. He replaced the "four roots" with "infinite seeds." Each of these "seeds" is something like an "element" in today's chemistry; so in some ways, this all sounds very modern. Every object in the world contains seeds of all elements, and in each object, the seeds of one element predominate.

"In all things, there is a portion of everything . . . For how could hair come from what is not hair? Or flesh from what is not flesh?"

Anaxagoras agreed with Empedocles that some force explaining motion and change was required, but he replaced Empedocles' all too mythical figures of Love and Strife with one force, a mental one, which he called "NOUS," or Mind. This means that the universe is organized according to an intelligent, rational order. Anaxagoras's NOUS is

almost like a god who creates objects out of the "seeds," or elements.

Furthermore, there is a distinction between the animate and the inanimate world in that the organic world contains Nous within it as a self-ordering principle, whereas the inorganic world is ordered externally by Nous. Nous itself is qualitatively identical everywhere, but its abilities are determined by the nature of the body that contains it. Humans aren't any smarter than carrots, but they can <u>do</u> more than carrots because they have tongues, opposable thumbs, and legs. (<u>You</u> wouldn't act very smart either if you were shaped like a carrot.)

Notice that this is the first time that something has been introduced to distinguish clearly between living substance and

"dead" matter. The anthropomorphic concept Nous looked somewhat promising to early philosophers, but eventually it disappointed them. Socrates said that at first he found it an exciting idea that ended up meaning nothing at all, and Aristotle said that Anaxagoras "stood out like a sober man from the random talkers that had preceded him," but later Aristotle was disillusioned by Anaxagoras, who "uses

Mind as a **deus ex machina** to account for the formation of the world; and whenever he is at a loss to explain why anything necessarily is, he drags it in. But in other cases he makes anything rather than mind the cause."

Precisely because Anaxagoras's view was anthropomorphic, it was still too mythical for Anaxagoras's successors, a group of philosophers led by LEUCIPPUS (ca. 460 B.C.–?) and DEMOCRITUS (ca. 460 b.c.–ca. 370 B.C.) known as "the atomists."

They saw the world as composed of material bodies, which themselves were composed of groups of "atoms." The Greek word ατομον means "indivisible," that which cannot be split.

Democritus made each atom a little piece of "Parmenidean Being" (uncreated, indestructible, eternal, indivisible, containing no "holes") and set them moving through empty space traversing absolutely necessary paths that were determined by rigid natural laws.

So, contrary to Parmenides view, both empty space and motion were real. Moreover, like atoms themselves, motion and space were "natural" and basic, admitting of no further analysis. It is the appearance of <u>inertia</u> and not that of motion that needs explaining, and Democritus's explanation, like that of Heraclitus, is that inertia is an illusion. That is to say, it is explained away. Thus, by the year 370 B.C., Greek philosophy had been led to a thoroughgoing **materialism** and a rigorous **determinism**. There was nothing in the world but material bodies in motion and there was no freedom, only necessity.

What had the pre-Socratic philosophers achieved? In them, a special kind of thinking had broken free from its mythical and religious ancestors, developing its own methods and content—a kind of thinking that would soon evolve into what today we know as science and philosophy. Looking back at the pre-Socratics, <u>WE</u> see a direct lineage between them and the great thinkers of our own time: the dichotomy between reason and the senses that Kant was to resolve in the eighteenth century was first made clear by the pre-Socratics; the first attempt to formulate a theory of evolution was made by them; and the first effort to solve the riddle of how mathematical numbers hold sway over the flux of reality—all this we see as a more or less unbroken genealogy from their time to ours.

But to the Greeks of the fifth century, the pre-Socratic philosophers had left a legacy of confusion.

The only thing the philosophers had succeeded in doing was to undermine the traditional religious and moral values, leaving nothing substantial in their place. (As Aristophanes said, "When Zeus is toppled, chaos succeeds him, and whirlwind rules.")

Besides, "the times they were a' changin'," socially and politically as well as intellectually. The old aristocracy, dedicated to the noble values of the Homeric legends, was losing ground to a new mercantile class, which was no longer interested in the virtues of Honor, Courage, and Fidelity but in Power and Success. How to achieve these in an incipient democracy? Through politics. And the access to political power was then, as it is today, through the study of rhetoric (read "law")—the art of swaying the masses with eloquent, though not necessarily truthful, argumentation.

II.
THE ATHENIAN
PERIOD

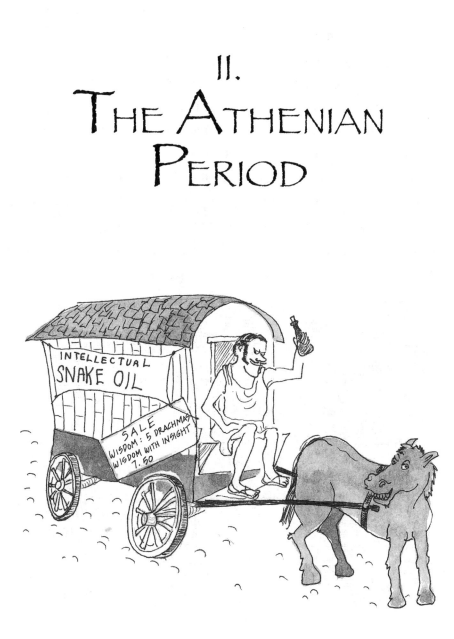

No surprise, then, that the next group of "philosophers" were not really philosophers as such but were rhetoricians who became known as SOPHISTS ("wise guys"). They traveled from city to city, charging admission to their lectures—lectures not on the nature of reality or truth but on the nature of power and persuasion. Not just skepticism but cynicism became the rule of the day. Perhaps the most famous (and least cynical) of the Sophists was PROTAGORAS (ca. 490–ca. 422 B.C.). He taught that the way to achieve success was through a careful and prudent acceptance of traditional customs—not because they were <u>true</u>, but because an understanding and manipulation of them is expedient. Far from being "true," for Protagoras all customs were relative, not absolute. In fact, <u>everything</u> is relative to human subjectivity. Protagoras's famous claim is "HOMO MENSURA"—Man is the measure.

Man is the measure of all things, of things that are, that they are, and of things that are not, that they are not.

Protagoras's emphasis on subjectivity, **relativism**, and expediency is the backbone of all sophism. According to some stories, Protagoras was indicted for blasphemy, and his book on the gods was burned publicly in Athens—

yet one of the few remaining
fragments of his concerning
religion states . . . ——→

Another famous
Sophist was
GORGIAS (ca.
483–375 B.C.).
He seems to have
wanted to dethrone
philosophy and
replace it with rhetoric.
In his lectures and in a
book he wrote, he "proved"
the following theses:

1. There is nothing.
2. If there were anything, no one could know it.
3. If anyone did know it, no one could communicate it.

The point, of course, is that if you can "prove" these
absurdities, you can "prove" anything.

Yet another Sophist was THRASYMACHUS, who is known for the claim, "Justice is in the interest of the stronger." That is to say, MIGHT MAKES RIGHT. According to him, all disputation about morality is empty, except insofar as it is reducible to a struggle for power.

According to the accounts handed down to us, two of the most cynical Sophists were CALLICLES and CRITIAS.

Callicles claimed that traditional morality is just a clever way for the weak masses to shackle the strong individual. He taught that the strong should throw off these shackles and that doing so would be somehow "naturally right." What matters is POWER, not justice. But why is power good? Because it is conducive to SURVIVAL. And why is survival good? Because it allows us to seek PLEASURE— pleasure in food, drink, and sex. This is what the enlightened man aims at, qualitatively and quantitatively. The traditional Greek virtue of <u>moderation</u> is for the simple and the feeble.

Critias (who was to become the cruelest of the Thirty Tyrants, who overturned the democracy and temporarily established an oligarchical dictatorship) taught that the clever ruler controls his subjects by encouraging their fear of nonexistent gods.

So we see that the essence of sophism is comprised of **subjectivism**, **skepticism**, and **nihilism**. Everything the pre-Socratics stood for is devalued. There is no objective reality, and if there were, the human mind could not fathom it. What matters is not truth but manipulation and expediency. No wonder Socrates was so offended by sophism.

Yet we must say a few kind words about sophism despite its negativism. First, many of the Sophists were

skilled politicians who actually contributed to the history of democracy. Second, history's animosity toward them is based mostly on reports we have of them from Socrates and Plato, who were enemies of the Sophists. Third, and most important, sophism had the positive effect of making the human being self-conscious. In pre-Socratic philosophy, there was no special consideration of the human. Suddenly, with Protagoras's "man is the measure," the human becomes interested in himself.

« »

The Sophists, who were professional teachers, met their match in a man who was possibly the greatest teacher of all time, SOCRATES (469–399 B.C.). Despite his overall disagreement with them, Socrates followed the Sophists' lead in turning away from the study of the cosmos and concentrating on the case of the human. But unlike the way the Sophists discoursed about the human being, Socrates wanted to base all argumentation on objectively valid definitions. To say "man is the measure" is saying very little if one does not know what "man" is.

I am surprised that Protagoras did not say that a pig, or a dog-faced baboon, is the measure of all things.

Socrates' discourse moved in two directions—outward, to objective definitions, and inward, to discover the inner person, the soul, which, for Socrates, was the source of all truth. Such a search was not to be conducted at a weekend lecture but was the quest of a lifetime.

Truth (trōōth): verity, conformity with fact. Honesty, integrity.

Socrates was hardly ever able to answer the questions he asked. Nevertheless, the query had to continue, for, as we know from his famous dictum . . .

"The unexamined life is not worth living."

Socrates spent much of his time in the streets and marketplace of Athens, querying every man he met about whether that man knew anything. Socrates said that, if there was an afterlife, he would pose the same question to the shades in Hades.

Ironically, Socrates himself professed to know nothing. The oracle at Delphi said that <u>therefore</u> Socrates was the wisest of all men. Socrates at least <u>knew</u> that he knew nothing, whereas the others falsely believed themselves to know something.

Socrates himself wrote no books, but his conversations were remembered by his disciple Plato and later published by him as dialogues. The typical Socratic dialogue has three divisions:

(1) A problem is posed (e.g., the problem of what virtue is, or justice, or truth, or beauty); Socrates becomes excited and enthusiastic to find someone who claims to know something.

(2) Socrates finds "minor flaws" in his companion's definition and slowly begins to unravel it, forcing his partner to admit his ignorance. (In one dialogue, Socrates' target actually ends up in tears.)

(3) An agreement is reached by the two admittedly ignorant men to pursue the truth seriously. Almost all the dialogues end inconclusively. Of course, they must do so. Socrates cannot give his disciple the truth. Each of us must find it out for ourselves.

In his quest for truth, Socrates managed to offend many of the powerful and pompous figures of Athens. His enemies conspired against him, getting him indicted for teaching false doctrines, for impiety, and for corrupting the youth. They brought him to trial hoping to humiliate him by forcing him to grovel and beg for mercy.

Far from groveling, at his trial Socrates humbled his prosecutors and angered the unruly jury of 500 by lecturing to them about their ignorance. Furthermore, when asked to suggest his own punishment, Socrates recommended that the Athenians build a statue in his honor and place it in the main square. The enraged jury condemned him to death by a vote of 280 to 220.

Ashamed of their act and embarrassed that they were about to put to death their most eminent citizen, the Athenians were prepared to look the other way when Socrates' prison guard was bribed to allow Socrates to escape.

**The Death of Socrates
(Vaguely After Jacques-Louis David, 1787)**

Despite the pleas of his friends, Socrates refused to do so, saying that if he broke the law by escaping, he would be declaring himself an enemy of all laws. So he drank the hemlock and philosophized with his friends to the last moment. In death, he became the universal symbol of martyrdom for the Truth.

« »

The most important of Socrates' young disciples was PLATO (427–347 B.C.), who was one of the most powerful thinkers in history. He is also the founder of the first university, "the Academy," where students read as exercises the Socratic dialogues, which he had written.

Plato

Because of his authorship, it is often difficult to distinguish between the thought of Socrates and that of Plato. In general, we can say that Plato's philosophy was more metaphysical, more systematic, and more "other-worldly" than Socrates' philosophy.

Plato's philosophy is introduced allegorically in the "Myth of the Cave," which appears in his most important work, *The Republic*. There he has Socrates conceive the following vision: Imagine prisoners chained in such a way that they face the back wall of a cave. There they have been for life and can see nothing of themselves or of each other. They see only shadows on the wall of the cave.

These shadows are cast by a fire that burns on a ledge above and behind them. Between the fire and the prisoners, there is a wall-lined path along which people walk

carrying vases, statues, and other artifacts on their heads. The prisoners hear the echoes of voices and see the shadows of the artifacts, and they mistake these echoes and shadows for reality.

Plato has Socrates imagine that one prisoner is unchained, turned around, and forced to look at the true source of the shadows. But the fire pains his eyes. He prefers the pleasant deception of the shadows.

Behind and above the fire is the mouth of the cave, and outside in the bright sunlight (only a little of which trickles into the cave) are trees, rivers, mountains, and sky.

Now the former prisoner is forced "up the steep and rugged ascent" (Plato's allegory of education) and brought to the sunlit exterior world. But the light blinds him. He must first look at the shadows of the trees (he is used to shadows), then at the trees and mountains. Then finally he is able to see the sun itself (the allegory of enlightenment).

Plato suggests that if this enlightened man were to return to the cave, he would appear ridiculous because he would see sunspots everywhere and not be able to penetrate the darkness.

And if he tried to liberate his fellow prisoners, they would be so angry at him for disturbing their illusions that they would set upon him and kill him—a clear allusion to the death of Socrates.

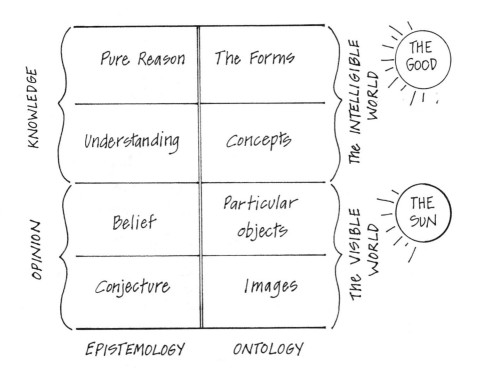

The allegory of the liberation of the slave, from darkness, deceit, and untruth and the hard journey into the light and warmth of the Truth, has inspired many philosophers and social leaders. But Plato meant it as more than just a poetic vision. He also gave it a precise technical application, seen in his "Simile of the Line," also found in *The Republic*. On the left side of the line we have an **epistemology** (theory of knowledge), on the right side, an **ontology** (theory of being). In addition, we have an implicit **ethics** (moral theory) and **aesthetics** (theory of beauty). The totality constitutes Plato's **metaphysics** (general worldview).

For each state of being (right side of the line), there is a corresponding state of awareness (left side). The lowest state of awareness is that of "conjecture," which has as its object "images," such as shadows and reflections (or images on the TV screen and video games).

The person in a state of conjecture mistakes an image for reality. This corresponds to the situation of the cave-bound prisoners watching the shadows.

The next level, that of "Belief," has as its object a particular thing—say, a particular horse or a particular act of justice. Like Conjecture, Belief still does not comprise knowledge but remains in the sphere of Opinion. This is because it is not yet conceptual but is grounded in the uncertainties of sense perception. (The person in a state of belief is like a prisoner who sees the artifact held above the wall inside the cave.)

"Opinion" and the objects of which it is aware are all sustained by the Sun. Without the Sun, there could be no horse and no image of a horse nor could we be aware of them in the absence of light.

For Opinion to become Knowledge, the particular object must be raised to the level of <u>theory</u>. (This stage, called

"Understanding" by Plato, corresponds to the status of the released prisoner looking at the shadows of the trees in the world above the cave.)

But according to Plato, theories and definitions are not empirical generalizations dependent on particular cases and abstracted from them. To the contrary, rather than coming from "below" on the Line, theories are themselves "images" of something higher—what Plato calls the **"Forms."** (In the same way that shadows and reflections are merely images of particular things, so theories or concepts are the "shadows" of the Forms.) When one beholds the Forms, one exercises Pure Reason, and one is like the liberated prisoner who gazed upon the trees and mountains in the sunlit upper world.

The
Form of
Beauty

The
Concept of
Beauty

Individual
Beautiful
Entities

Imitations of
Beautiful Entities
(paintings, photos,
reflections,
shadows)

Plato's conception of the Forms is very complicated, but we can simplify it by saying that they are the eternal truths that are the source of all Reality. Consider, for example, the concept of beauty. Things in the sensible world are beautiful to the extent that they "imitate" or "participate" in Beauty. However, these beautiful things will break, grow old, or die. But Beauty itself (the Form) is eternal. It will always be. The same can be said of Truth and Justice. (Also, more embarrassingly, of Horseness or of Toothpickness.)

Furthermore, just as the sensible world and awareness of it are dependent on the Sun, so are the Forms and knowledge of them dependent on the Good, which is a Superform, or the Form of all Forms. The state of beholding the Good is represented in the myth of the cave by the released prisoner beholding the Sun itself. Plato's theory is such that the whole of Reality is founded upon the Good, which is Reality's source of being. And all Knowledge is ultimately knowledge of the Good.

Moreover, Plato optimistically holds that if one ever comes to know the Good, one becomes good. Ignorance is the only sin. No one would willingly do wrong.

How can we learn the Truth? Where can we find the Forms and the Good? Who can teach us? Plato had curious answers to these questions. In the dialogue called *Meno*, Plato had an unschooled slaveboy solve a difficult mathematical problem by answering affirmatively or negatively a series of simple questions posed by Socrates. Plato concluded from this episode that the slaveboy always knew the

answer but didn't know that he knew. All truth comes from within—from the soul. One's immortal soul is born with the truth, having beheld the Forms in their purity before its embodiment. Birth, or the embodiment of the soul, is so traumatic that one forgets what one knows and must spend the rest of life plumbing the depths of the soul to recover what one already knows. Hence, Plato's strange doctrine that all Knowledge is recollection. Now we see Socrates' role as that of helping his student to remember, just as does the psychoanalyst with his or her patient today. (Plato's theory of recollection is the source of the Freudian conception of the unconscious.)

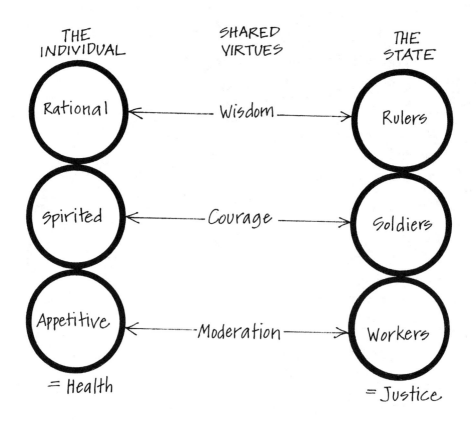

THE INDIVIDUAL	SHARED VIRTUES	THE STATE
Rational	← Wisdom →	Rulers
Spirited	← Courage →	Soldiers
Appetitive	← Moderation →	Workers
= Health		= Justice

The Republic is well known not only for its epistemology but also for its social philosophy. The latter for Plato is a combination of psychology and political science. He said that the City (the "Republic") is the individual writ large. Just as the individual's psyche has three aspects—(1) the appetitive, animal side, (2) the spirited source of action, and (3) the rational aspect—so does the ideal City have three classes—(1) the workers and the artisans, (2) the soldiers, and (3) the rulers. In the psyche, the rational part must convince the spirited part to help it control the appetitive. Otherwise, there will be an unbalanced soul, and neurosis will ensue.

Similarly, in the City, the rulers must be philosophers who have beheld the Forms, hence who know what is good. They must train the military caste to help control the naturally unruly peasants. The latter will be allowed to use money, own property, and wear decorations in moderation, but the members of the top two classes, who understand the corrupting effect of greed, will live in an austere, absolute communism, sleeping and eating together, owning no property, receiving no salary, and having sexual relations on a prearranged schedule with partners shared by all. These rules will guarantee that the City will not be frenzied and anarchic—a strange beginning for the discipline of Political Science (one from which it has still not recovered)!

The members of the ideal City will be allowed to play simple lyres and pipes and sing patriotic, uplifting songs, but most artists will be drummed out of the Republic. This is for four reasons: (1) Ontological: Since art deals with images (the lowest rung in the Simile of the Line), art is an imitation of an imitation. (Art is "thrice removed from the throne.") (2) Epistemological: The artist is at the conjectural stage. He knows nothing but <u>claims</u> to know something. (3) Aesthetical: Art expresses itself in sensual images, hence distracts us from Beauty itself, which is purely spiritual. (4) Moral: Art is created by and appeals to the appetite side of the soul (Freud's ID). Art is either erotic or violent or both, hence it is an incitement to anarchy. Even Homer must be censored.

(The whole enterprise of The Republic can be viewed as a plea that philosophy take over the role that art had hitherto played in Greek culture.)

Plato did not live to see the inauguration of his ideal state, nor to see the installation of a Philosopher King who would know the Good, but the legacy that Plato left is still very much with us, for better or for worse. The eminent British-American philosopher Alfred North Whitehead once said that the history of philosophy is merely a series of footnotes to *The Republic*.

« »

Plato's influence is clearly seen in the thought of one of his best students, ARISTOTLE (384–322 B.C.). Aristotle, born in Stagira, spent 20 years at Plato's academy. Soon after the death of the master, Aristotle left the school because of disagreements with its new chiefs, and he founded an academy of his own, the Lyceum. In Aristotle's school, Platonic philosophy was taught, but it was also criticized.

Mere Dog Copies

The main thrust of Aristotle's dispute with his mentor concerned the latter's "other-worldliness." For Plato, there are two worlds: the unspeakably lofty world of Forms, and the world of mere "things," which is but a poor imitation of the former. Aristotle contradicted this view, asserting that there is only ONE world, and that we are right smack in the middle of it. In criticizing Plato, Aristotle asked: If Forms are essences of things, how can they exist separated from things? If they are the <u>cause</u> of things, how can they exist in a different world? And a most telling criticism has to do with the problem of CHANGE and MOTION, which the early Greeks had tried to solve.

Parmenidean
Permanence

Heraclitian
Hustle

They thought that either stability was an illusion (the view of Heraclitus, for example) or that motion was an illusion (the view of Parmenides). Plato had tried to resolve the dilemma by acknowledging the insights of both Heraclitus and Parmenides. The former's world is the unstable and transient realm of the visible. The latter's world is the immutable realm of the intelligible composed of the eternally unchanging Forms, which themselves are poorly reflected in the transitory world of the Visible. But did Plato's compromise really solve the problem of motion and change? Is it really comprehensible to explain "changing things" by saying that they are bad imitations of unchanging things?

Aristotle thought not.

In offering his own solution to the problem, Aristotle employed some of the same terminology as Plato. He said that a distinction must be drawn between FORM and MATTER, but that these two features of reality can be distinguished only in thought, not in fact. Forms are not separate entities. They are embedded in particular things.

They are IN the world. To think otherwise is an intellectual confusion. A particular object, to count as an object at all, must have both form and matter. Form, as Plato had said, is UNIVERSAL, in the sense that many particulars can have the same form. Aristotle called an object's form its "WHATNESS." That is, when you say what something is (it's a tree, it's a book), you are naming its form. The form is a thing's "essence," or "nature." It is related to the thing's FUNCTION (a wheel, a knife, a brick, etc.).

An object's MATTER is what is unique to that object. Aristotle called it the object's "THISNESS." All wheels or trees have the same form (or function), but no two have the same matter. Matter is "the principle of individuation." An object with both form and matter is what Aristotle called a **substance**. His anti-Platonic metaphysics holds that reality is composed of a plurality of substances. It is not composed of an upper tier of eternal Forms and a lower tier of matter that unsuccessfully attempts to imitate those Forms. This is Aristotle's **pluralism** as opposed to Plato's **dualism** (a dualism that verges on **idealism** because, for Plato, the most "real" tier of reality is the nonmaterial). How does Aristotle's pluralism solve the problem of motion and change, a problem that was unsuccessfully addressed by his predecessors? It does so by reinterpreting MATTER and FORM as POTENTIALITY and ACTUALITY and by turning these concepts into a theory of change. Any object in the world can be analyzed in terms of these categories.

Aristotle's famous example is that of an acorn. The acorn's matter contains the potentiality of becoming an oak tree, which is the acorn's actuality. The acorn is the potentiality of there being an oak tree. The oak tree is the actuality of the acorn. So, for Aristotle, "form" is an operating cause. Each individual substance is a self-contained **teleological** (i.e., goal-oriented) system.

In fact, Aristotle analyzed all substances in terms of four causes: The material cause is the "stuff" out of which something is made (e.g., a chunk of marble that is to become a statue). The formal cause is the form, or essence, of the statue, that which it strives to be. (This exists both in the mind of the artist and potentially in the marble itself.) The efficient cause is the actual force that brings about the change (the sculptor's chipping the block of stone). The <u>final</u> <u>cause</u> is the ultimate purpose of the object (the beauty of the Parthenon).

Nature, then, is a teleological system in which each substance is striving for self-actualization and for whatever perfection is possible within the limitations allowed it by its particular essence. As in Plato's theory, everything is striving unconsciously toward "the Good." Aristotle believed that for such a system to work, some concrete perfection must actually exist as the TELOS (or goal) toward which all things are striving.

This entity Aristotle called "the Prime Mover." It serves as a kind of god in Aristotle's metaphysics, but unlike the traditional gods of Greece and unlike the God of Western religion, the Prime Mover is almost completely nonanthropomorphic. It is the cause of the universe, not in the Judeo-Christian sense of creating it out of nothing, but in the sense of a Final Cause; everything "moves" toward it in the way a runner moves toward a goal. The Prime Mover is the only thing in the universe with no potentiality because, being perfect, it cannot change. It is pure actuality, which is to say, pure activity. What activity?

The activity of pure thought. And what does it think about? Perfection! That is to say, about itself. The Prime Mover's knowledge is immediate, complete self-consciousness. —What we seem to have here is an absolutely divine case of narcissism.

Aristotle's **moral philosophy**, as it appears in his manuscript now called *The Nicomachean Ethics*, reflects his teleological metaphysics. The notion of goal, or purpose, is the overriding one in his moral theory. Aristotle noted that every act is performed for some purpose, which he defined as the "good"

of that act. (We perform an act because we find its purpose to be worthwhile.) Either the totality of our acts is an infinitely circular series (we get up in order to eat breakfast, we eat breakfast in order to go to work, we go to work in order to get money, we get money so we can buy food in order to be able to eat breakfast, etc., etc., etc.), in which case life would be a pretty meaningless endeavor. Or there is some ultimate good toward which the purposes of all acts are directed. If there is such a good, we should try to come to know it so that we can adjust all our acts toward it in order to avoid that saddest of all tragedies—the wasted life.

According to Aristotle, there is general verbal agreement that the end toward which all human acts are directed is happiness; therefore, happiness is the human good since we seek happiness for its own sake, not for the sake of something else. But unless we philosophize about happiness and get to know exactly what it is and how to achieve it, it will be platitudinous simply to <u>say</u> that happiness is the ultimate good. To determine the nature of happiness, Aristotle turned to his metaphysical schema and asked, "What is the function of the human?" (in the same way he would ask about the function of a knife or an acorn). He came to the conclusion that a human's function is to engage in "an activity of the soul which is in accordance with virtue and which follows a rational principle." Before grasping this complicated definition, we must determine what "virtue" is and what kinds of virtues there are. But first, as an aside, it must be mentioned that Aristotle believed that certain material conditions must hold before happiness can be achieved.

This list of conditions will reveal Aristotle's elitism: We need good friends, riches, and political power. We need a good birth, good children, and good looks (". . . for the man who is very ugly in appearance . . . is not very likely to be happy"). We must not be very short. Furthermore, we must be free from the need of performing manual labor. ("No man can practice virtue who is living the life of a mechanic or laborer.")—It should be noted that Aristotle's moral theory would be left substantially intact if his elitist bias were deleted.

Now, as to virtues, there are two kinds: intellectual and moral. Intellectual virtues are acquired through a combination of inheritance and education, and moral virtues through imitation, practice, and habit. The habits that we

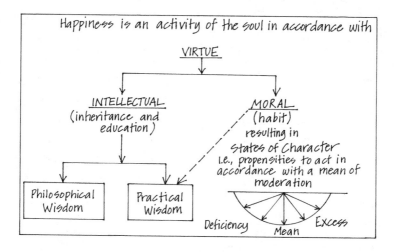

develop result in "states of character," that is, in dispositions to act certain ways, and these states of character are "virtuous" for Aristotle if they result in acts that are in accordance with a "golden mean" of moderation. For example, when it comes to facing danger, one can act with excess, that is, show too much fear. (This is cowardice.) Or one can act deficiently by showing too little fear. (This is foolhardiness.) Or one can act with moderation, and hence virtuously, by showing the right amount of fear. (This is courage.) Aristotle realized that the choices we must make if we are to learn moral virtue cannot be made mathematically; rather, they are always context-bound and must be approached through trial and error.

Returning to the intellectual virtues of practical and philosophical wisdom, the former is the wisdom necessary to make judgments consistent with one's understanding of the good life. It is therefore related to moral virtue (as in the diagram). Philosophical wisdom is scientific, disinterested, and contemplative. It is associated with pure reason, and, for Aristotle, the capacity for reason is that which is most human; therefore, philosophical wisdom is the highest virtue. So, when Aristotle defined happiness as "an activity of the soul in accordance with virtue," the activity referred to is philosophical activity. The human being can only be happy by leading a contemplative life, but not a monastic one. We are not only philosophical animals but also social ones. We are engaged in a world where decisions concerning practical matters are forced upon us constantly. Happiness (hence the good life) requires excellence in both spheres.

Not only did Aristotle make major contributions to metaphysics and ethics, he also wrote important treatises on aesthetics and politics. Furthermore, he singlehandedly founded the science of **logic**, that is, the science of valid inference. Symbolic logic has developed a long way since Aristotle's time, but it is indebted to him as its founder, and it has made more additions than corrections to his work.

Some of Aristotle's empirical claims about the world leave something to be desired (for instance, his claim that falling rocks accelerate because they are happy to be getting home, or his claim that snakes have no testicles because they have no legs). Nevertheless, Aristotle's metaphysics, his ethics, his logic, and his aesthetics remain permanent monuments to the greatness of human thought.

Daddy!   ??

III.
THE HELLENISTIC PERIOD

After the death of Aristotle, Greek civilization entered what historians call the Hellenistic era. It is a period of cultural decline. The Greek city-states, unable to solve the problem of political unity, were decimated by the Peloponnesian War and ravaged by the plague. First they fell under Macedonian rule, then, after the death of Alexander the Great, eventually were absorbed into the newly emerging Roman Empire. Many of the philosophies of this "decadent" period began in Greece but received their greatest exposure in Rome. This is true of the two major philosophies of the period, epicureanism and stoicism.

The philosophy of Epicurus (341–270 B.C.) is known (not surprisingly) as EPICUREANISM. If today the term hints of gluttony, debauchery, and bacchanalian orgies, that is not Epicurus's fault but the fault of some of his Roman interpreters;

Epicurus himself led a life of sobriety and simplicity; eating bread, cheese, and olives; drinking a bit of wine; napping in his hammock; and enjoying conversation with his friends while strolling through his garden. He died with dignity and courage after a painful, protracted disease.

The Individual in the Roman Empire

Epicureanism was grounded in the atomic theory of Democritus, but in fact, Epicurus, like all post-Alexandrian philosophers, does not seem to have been really interested in science but in finding out about the good life. However, since Aristotle's time, the notion of "the good life" had suffered a setback. It no longer made sense to advocate being active, influential, political, and responsible as a way of self-improvement. Reality seemed to be unmoved by personal initiative, and the individual himself was developing a feeling of powerlessness as he was about to be absorbed into the massive, impersonal bureaucracy of the Roman

Empire. Like Aristotle, Epicurus believed that the goal of life was happiness, but happiness he equated simply with PLEASURE. No act should be undertaken except for the pleasure in which it results, and no act should be rejected except for the pain that it produces. This provoked Epicurus to analyze the different kinds of pleasure. There are two kinds of desires, hence two kinds of pleasure as a result of gratifying those desires: NATURAL DESIRE (which has two subclasses) and VAIN DESIRE:

I. Natural desire
   A. Necessary (e.g., desire for food and sleep)
   B. Unnecessary (e.g., desire for sex)
II. Vain desire (e.g., the desire for decorative clothing or exotic food)

Natural necessary desires <u>must</u> be satisfied and are easy to satisfy. They result in a good deal of pleasure and in very few painful consequences. Vain desires do not need

The Pursuit of Vain Pleasure

to be satisfied and are not easy to satisfy. Because there are no natural limits to them, they tend to become obsessive and lead to very painful consequences.

The desire for sex is natural but usually can be overcome; and when it can be, it should be because satisfaction of the sexual drive gives intense pleasure. But it involves one in relationships that are usually ultimately more painful than pleasant, and are often extremely painful.

One of the natural and necessary desires to which Epicurus pays a great deal of attention is the desire for <u>repose</u>. This is to be understood both physically and psychically. The truly good person (i.e., the one who experiences the most pleasure) is the one who, having overcome all unnecessary desires, gratifies his necessary desires in the most moderate way possible, leaves plenty of time for physical and mental repose, and is free from worry.

We will notice that Epicurus's definition of pleasure is <u>negative</u>, that is, pleasure is the absence of pain. It is this negative definition that prevents Epicurus from falling into a crass sensualism. The trouble with this definition is that, taken to its logical extremity, the <u>absence</u> of life is better

Beyond the Pleasure Principle

than any life at all (as Freud discovered in his *Beyond the Pleasure Principle*, where he claimed that behind the "pleasure principle" is THANATOS, the Death instinct).

This is a bit ironic since Epicurus himself had claimed that his philosophy dispelled the fear of death. Democritus's atomism led Epicurus to believe that death was merely the absence of sensation and consciousness; therefore, there could be no sensation or consciousness of death to fear. "Where death is, we are not. Where we are, death is not."

Some of Epicurus's Roman followers interpreted "plea-sure" quite differently, defining it as a positive titillation. It is because of these extremists that today epicureanism is often associated with sensualistic **hedonism**. Sickly Epicurus, swinging in his hammock, would have disapproved. (Though not too harshly. Polemics cause agitation, which is painful.) Epicurus's theory never constituted a major philo-sophical movement, but he had disciples in both Greece and Rome for a number of centuries. His most famous fol-lower was the Roman LUCRETIUS, who, in the first century B.C., wrote a long poem, *On the Nature of Things*, expounding the philosophy of his master. It is through Lucretius's poem that many have been introduced to the thoughts of Epicurus.

STOICISM was another important Hellenistic philosophy which was transported to Rome. It was founded in Greece by ZENO of CYPRUS (334–262 B.C.), who used to preach to his students from a portico, or "stoa" (hence the term <u>stoicism</u>, literally, "Porchism"). Like epicureanism, stoicism had its roots in pre-Socratic materialism, but stoicism too, especially in its Roman form, became uninterested in physics and peculiarly concerned with the problem of human conduct. The three most interesting of the Roman stoics were SENECA (A.D. 4–65), a dramatist and high-ranking statesman; EPICTETUS (late first century A.D.), a slave who earned his freedom; and MARCUS AURELIUS (A.D. 121–180), a Roman emperor. (It's quite striking that a slave and an emperor could share the same philosophy of resignation, though probably this was easier for the

Zeno at the Stoa

emperor than for the slave!) The stoics accepted the Socratic equation, "virtue = knowledge." There is a cognitive state that, once achieved, guarantees complete well-being. One should strive throughout one's life to acquire this wisdom. Human excellence is attained instantaneously once one has gained the enlightenment.

The duration of such a life of perfection is indifferent (which fact leads to the stoic advocacy of suicide under certain circumstances). To achieve this state of blessedness, one must free oneself from all worldly demands, particularly those of the emotions and of pleasure-seeking. The stoic wise man is an ascete. He has transcended the passions that create a disorderly condition in the soul. The stoic has no interest in all those objects that excite the passions of grief, joy, hope, or fear in normal human beings.

What is the content of stoic wisdom? It is similar to the Aristotelian notion that the good consists of acting in accordance with one's nature. The stoic addition to this idea is that to so act requires acting in accordance with nature itself, that is, with the totality of reality (which the stoics take to be divine). Considered as a whole, reality is perfect. Humans will also become perfect if they learn to live in accordance with the divine plan of reality. This requires that one make one's desires identical with the overall providential plan for the universe. In fact, a person can do <u>nothing</u> <u>but</u> conform to the grand design, and stoic wisdom consists in recognizing this truth. Fools are those who try to impose their own selfish desires on reality. This results in unhappiness and unfreedom. If **freedom** is the unity of will and ability (i.e., being able to do what one wants), then the only way to be free is to want what the universe wants. We shouldn't wish that we could get what we desire, rather we should desire what we get. If we could learn to equate what we want with what's the case, then

Don't Try to Get What You Want—Rather Want What You Get

we would always be free and happy, since we'd always get just what we want. This is stoic wisdom.

The stoics realized that if one ever achieved this lofty state, the apparent harshness of reality might jeopardize one's inner equilibrium, and one might backslide into pain and anxiety. For this reason, and because the stoics believed that the amount of time one spent in the enlightened state was indifferent, the stoics advocated suicide under certain conditions. Epictetus said of suicide, "Tis smokey and I go away." Seneca said, "The dirtiest death is preferable to the daintiest slavery" and, "To die well is to escape the danger of living badly." In fact, on the advice of the Emperor Nero, Seneca did step into the bath and open his veins.

This way down

During the period when stoicism was exercising its greatest influence, a new social and religious form of thought was coming to the fore: Christianity. And although the Christians had not learned to defend their new religion with a systematic philosophy as they would in the Middle Ages, their doctrine was in competition with the philosophies of the day for the hearts and minds of men and women. All such thought systems were responding to the same problems, so it is no surprise that there are some

similarities between Christianity and a philosophy like stoicism; for example, both philosophies share the doctrine of
resignation, the disdain for attachment to earthly things,
and the concern with conforming to the will of divine
Providence. (The differences cannot be overlooked, however,
such as the discrepancy between stoic and Christian
teachings on suicide. Also, stoicism was inclined to be qui-
etistic and acquiescent to political authority, whereas in
its inception Christianity tended to be activistic and resis-
tant to political domination.

Epictetus said, "Take no oath, or . . . take only as many
as you must." This attitude contrasts greatly with that of
many Christians who refused to swear an oath on the divinity of the emperor and were martyred for that refusal.)

≪ ≫

After the death of the stoic Marcus Aurelius ("the
last good emperor"), a long period of upheaval and disorder
ensued. The helplessness that people felt in the face of

the decadence of the crumbling empire was responded to by a religious revival. The most prominent philosophical religious competitor with Christianity during the third century A.D. was a mystical form of Platonism known today as NEO-PLATONISM, espoused by PLOTINUS (204–270). We have already seen a deep-seated propensity toward other-worldliness in Plato, which Aristotle had criticized. Plato's claim of superiority for the other world fit in well with the world-weariness of the third century.

For Plotinus, as for Plato before him, absolute truth and certainty cannot be found in this world. Plato had taught a purely rational method for transcending the flux of the world and achieving truth and certainty, but Plotinus preached that such a vision can only be achieved extra-rationally, through a kind of ecstatic union with the One. The One was for Plotinus the Absolute, or God. Nothing can be truly known about the One in any rational sense, nor can any characterization of the One be strictly correct. If we review Plato's Simile of the Line from a Plotinian perspective, we will see that language, and therefore thought, function by drawing <u>distinctions</u> (we say "this is a pen," meaning it is <u>not</u> the desk); but in the One, no distinctions exist, hence nothing can be thought or said

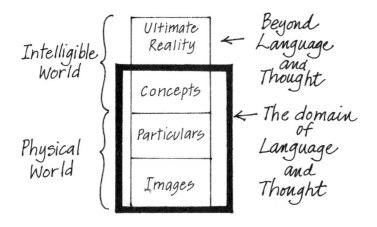

about it. A person can know the One only by uniting with it. That can be done in this life in moments of mystical rapture, but in the long run the goal can only be achieved in death.

One can prepare for the ultimate union through an ascetic program of virtuous living. Plotinus's own version of "the Line" is based on his idea that God, or the Absolute, does not perform acts of creation (that would sully God's unchangeableness), rather God "emanates." That is, God is reflected onto lower planes, and these reflections represent kinds of imitations of God's perfection in descending degrees of fragmentation. (What we have here is a kind of "gooey" Simile of the Line.) This metaphysics borders on **pantheism**—the view that reality and God are the same.

Because the philosophy of Plotinus and his followers was the last philosophy of the classical period, his version of Platonism was the one that was handed down to the medieval world. Because of this fact, we will see that the problem of pantheism crops up again in the Middle Ages, this time not to haunt the death scene of classicism but the birth scene of Christian philosophy.

IV.
MEDIEVAL
PHILOSOPHY

In the year A.D. 313, the Roman Emperor Constantine was converted to Christianity, and, even though only one in ten citizens of the empire was a Christian, Christianity became the official religion of the realm. During the next couple of centuries, the early Church fathers turned to the prevailing neo-Platonic philosophical tradition in their search for intellectual foundations for their still relatively new religion. The first truly important philosopher in this Christian Platonic tradition was AUGUSTINE OF HIPPO (354–430). He had one foot squarely planted in the classical world and one in the medieval world, and he straddled the abyss that separated these two worlds.

As a young student of rhetoric in Rome, acutely aware of his own sensual nature, Augustine was concerned with the problem of good and evil. He became attracted to manicheanism (founded by Mani of Persia in the third century), which, combining certain Christian and Persian elements, was a philosophy that understood reality in terms of an eternal struggle between the principle of light (Good) and the principle of darkness (Evil). The strife between these two principles manifested itself as the world. The soul represented the good and the body represented evil. As a Manichee, Augustine could attribute his many sins to a principle somehow outside himself.

The Devil made me do it!

But Augustine soon became dissatisfied with this "solution" to the problem of evil, and he became attracted to neo-Platonism and its conception of an immaterial reality. It was from neo-Platonism that Augustine got his idea of evil not as a real feature of reality, but as a LACK, an incompleteness, a privation. (Recall the Simile of the Line:

the more goodness a thing has, the more real it is.
Conversely, the less reality it has, the worse it is. Just as
a dental cavity is a lack of calcium [a hole is not a thing,
it is an absence of being], so is a sin not a thing, but an
absence of goodness.) In 388, after a minor mystical experience, Augustine converted to Christianity and never again
vacillated in his intellectual commitment. In 391 he was
ordained priest and in 396 became the Bishop of Hippo, on
the North African coast. During this period, Christianity
was still seeking to achieve focus on its own identity, and
Augustine spent an enormous amount of energy combating
a series of heresies: **donatism**, **priscillianism**, **arianism**,
and, of course, that of his former persuasion,
manicheanism. But at the same time, he had to combat a
new and especially difficult heresy, that of pelagianism.
Pelagius's heresy was that of overaccentuating the role of
free will in salvation and minimizing the role of God's grace.
Much to Augustine's embarrassment, Pelagius had been
using Augustine's book on free will to defend his own view.

Does God's Foreknowledge Determine Our Actions?

So Augustine found himself walking a tightrope. He had to attack the manichees for minimizing free will and attack the Pelagians for overemphasizing it. This problem occupied him in some very subtle philosophical reasoning.

THE PROBLEM: If God is all-wise (omniscient), then he knows the future. If he knows the future, then the future must unfold exactly in accordance with his knowledge (otherwise, he does <u>not</u> know the future). If the events in the future <u>must</u> occur according to God's foreknowledge of them, then they are <u>necessary</u>, and there is no freedom. If there is no freedom, then humans are not responsible for their acts, in which case it would be immoral to punish people for their sins. (If God knew millions of years before Judas was born that he would betray Jesus, how could God send Judas to hell for his sin?) So the conclusion seems to be: Either God is omniscient but immoral, or he is benevolent but ignorant.

Judas

How can Augustine avoid this unpalatable dilemma? He does so with a number of sophisticated arguments. One is that, for God, there is no past or future, only an eternal present. For him, everything happens at once. To say "God knew millions of years before Judas's birth that he would betray Jesus" is to make the <u>human</u> error of believing that God is <u>in</u> time. In fact, God is outside of time. (That's what it means to say that God is eternal.) Another tack of Augustine's is to admit that God's knowledge of the world entails **necessity**, but to deny that necessity is incompatible with freedom. Like the stoics, Augustine believed that freedom is the capacity of doing what one wants, and one can do what one wants even if God (or anyone else) already knows what that person wants. Augustine pointed out that God's foreknowledge of a decision doesn't <u>cause</u> the decision, any more than my own acts are caused by my knowledge of what I'm going to do.

God Is Not in Time

This is a sample of Augustinian thought. His philosophy is a profound meditation on the relation between God and the human being. It was addressed to a troubled and expiring world. The old order was crumbling. In fact, on the same day Augustine succumbed to the infirmities of old age in the cathedral at Hippo, the barbaric Vandals were burning the city. Even though they left the cathedral standing out of respect for him, the fires that consumed Hippo were the same ones that consumed the Roman

Empire. The classical period was over, and that long night, which some call the Dark Ages, had commenced.

At the death of Augustine, Western philosophy fell into a state of deterioration that was to last for 400 years. This period, the advent of the medieval world, truly was the Dark Night of the Western soul. The Roman legions could no longer control the frontiers of the empire, and the Teutonic tribes from the eastern forest swarmed over the old empire.

Rome was sacked twice within a thirty-five-year period. The new "barbarian" emperors no longer bore Latin names but Germanic ones. They were not interested in culture as it has been known in classical times. Philosophy as the Greeks and Romans had understood it was in danger of perishing.

During this long dark night, philosophy flickered only as individual candle flames at distant corners of the old dead empire. Certain isolated monasteries in Italy, Spain, Britain, and on the rocky crags of islands in the Irish Sea produced what are known as the ENCYCLOPEDIASTS, who systematically compiled and conserved whatever remnants of classical wisdom they could lay their hands on. The three salient figures in this tradition are BOETHIUS (480–525) in Italy, ISIDORE (570–636) in Spain, and THE VENERABLE BEDE (674–735) in England. (St. Isidore's encyclopedia is particularly revealing. Under the letter "A" we find both an entry on the atomic theory and an entry on the Antipodes, a people who were supposed to inhabit the rocky plains of southern Africa and who, Isidore believed, had their big toes on the outside of the feet, thereby allowing them more maneuverability among the rocky fields where they dwelt!)

Isidore's hodge-podge is emblematic of the state of philosophy during the Dark Ages.

Suddenly, after four centuries of rel-

An Antipode Showing Off in Rocky Terrain

ative silence, philosophy blossomed forth in the work of the first great metaphysical system builder of the Middle Ages, the redundantly named JOHN SCOTUS ERIGENA ("John the Irishman, the Irishman" [ca. 810 – ca. 877]). John had been called from Ireland to the Palatine School of King Charles the Bald to translate the Greek document known today as "the Pseudo-Dionysius" (a work falsely believed to have been written by St. Paul's Christian convert, St. Dionysius, but believed today to have been written by a neo-Platonic philosopher unsympathetic to Christianity). Erigena's own book, *On the Divisions of Nature*, was greatly influenced by his reading of the "Pseudo-Dionysius" and is a confusing combination of Christian dogma and neo-Platonic pantheism. Through his book and his influential translation,

Platonism gained an even greater foothold in Christianity.

John's goal was the categorization and understanding of the totality of reality (what he calls "Nature"). The first categorical distinction he drew was between

| THINGS THAT ARE | and | THINGS THAT ARE NOT |

John Scotus Divides Up Nature

This distinction involves the Platonic supposition that there is a hierarchy of being, that some things are more real than other things. "Things that are not" are those entities that on a neo-Platonic scale contained a lesser degree of reality. For example, a particular tree or horse contains less being than the form "tree," or the form "horse," hence particulars are subsumed under this negative category. So are all "lacks" or "deprivations," such as sinful acts or acts of forgetting. The most surprising thing we find in this category is what John called "super-reality"—that which cannot be grasped by the human intellect, that which on the neo-Platonic scale is "beyond being." Apparently, John was talking about God.

What is left? What can be called "the things that are"? Only those entities that can be comprehended by pure human intellect, namely, the Platonic forms! All else is other than being.

So we find this Christian scholar in the apparently awkward position of claiming that God is among those things classified as nonexistent—in the same class where you would expect to find mountains made of gold, centaurs, griffins, and round squares. So why doesn't this end all discussion of God once and for all? Because John's method of the "vias affirmativa and negativa" (borrowed from the "Pseudo-Dionysius") allowed him to make sense of the nothingness of a being beyond being.

VIA AFFIRMATIVA	VIA NEGATIVA
We affirm: "God is wise." ↑	We deny the affirmation: "God is not wise." ↑
This affirmation is true only as metaphor. "Wisdom" is a word that gets its meaning from human discourse. We can apply it to God only analogically to give us a hint of his nature.	This negation is literal. Because "wisdom" gets its meaning from human discourse, it cannot literally apply to God.

This affirmation and its negation do not lead to a self-contradiction, rather they serve as thesis and antithesis and are dialectically reconciled in a (Hegelian-like) synthesis that will lead us to realize that God is somehow superwise. The same method will show us why John said that God does not exist but that he [super-] exists.

There is yet another way in which John Scotus Erigena divided Nature:

1. Nature that creates and is uncreated
2. Nature that creates and is created
3. Nature that is created and does not create
4. Nature that is not created and does not create

Item 1 = God.

Item 2 = the Platonic forms.

Item 3 = the physical world.

Item 4 = God.

(Remember, in this neo-Platonic schema, to say that something "X" creates is to say that there is something below X in the hierarchy of reality that is dependent upon X. Conversely, to say that something "Y" is created is to say that Y is dependent on something above it for its existence.)

In this system, God is both Alpha and Omega, Beginning and End, Creator and Goal of Creation. God issues out into the world and comes back to himself. All this looks suspiciously like Plotinus's pantheistic system of emanations, and though many attempts were made to defend The Divisions of Nature against the charge of

Alpha and Omega

heresy, eventually it was condemned as heterodoxical in 1225 by Pope Honorius III.

After John Scotus Erigena, there were no great systemmakers again for the next 350 years. From the ninth to the thirteenth century, philosophy would be done in a more piecemeal manner than it was done by Augustine or John Scotus, or than it would be in the thirteenth century by Thomas Aquinas. It was confined to a kind of philosophical grammar of theological terms. However, this does not mean that it was always unimpressive. One of the most striking pieces of philosophical logic produced in the medieval period is the proof of God's existence created by ANSELM of CANTERBURY (1033–1109), later <u>Saint</u> Anselm.

Anselm's argument began with a reference to the fool (of Psalms 53:1) who "says in his heart, 'There is no God.'" But, said Anselm, even the fool is convinced that something exists in the understanding at least, than which nothing greater can be conceived. For when he hears of this he understands it. . . . And assuredly that than which nothing greater can be conceived, cannot exist in the understanding alone. For suppose it exists in the understanding alone: then it can be conceived to exist in reality, which is greater. . . . Hence, there is no doubt that there exists a being than which nothing greater can be conceived, and it exists both in the understanding and in reality . . . and this being thou art, O Lord, our God.

Psalms 53:1

Try out Anselm's argument. Conceive in your mind the most perfect being you can think of. (Anselm believed it will look very much like the conception of the traditional Christian God—a being who is all-good, all-knowing, all-pow-erful, eternal, and unchangeable.) Now ask yourself, does the entity you conceived exist <u>only</u> in your mind? If it is even possible that it exists only there, then it is <u>not</u> the

One that exists only here is less perfect than One

who exists out here.

most perfect entity conceivable because such an entity who existed both in your mind and EXTRAMENTALLY would be even more perfect. Therefore, if it's possible even to conceive of a most perfect being, such a being necessarily exists.

This is a slippery argument, and it immediately found detractors. A contemporary of Anselm's, GAUNILON, a monk by profession, made the following objections on behalf of the fool.

1. It is, in fact, impossible to conceive of "a being than which nothing greater can be conceived." The very project boggles the mind.

2. If Anselm's argument were valid, then it would follow that the mere ability to conceive of a perfect tropical island would logically entail the existence of such an island.

Anselm's response was as simple as Gaunilon's rebuttle:

Gaunilon's Objections

1. If you understand the phrase "most perfect being," then you already have conceived of such a being.

2. There is nothing in the <u>definition</u> of a tropical island that entails perfection, but the very definition of God entails that he be all-perfect, so it is impossible to conceive of God as lacking a perfection; and since it is obviously more perfect to be than not to be, the bare conception of God entails his existence.

This argument is both more difficult and more ingenious than it may appear to you. It is, in fact, a very good argument (which is not to say that it is flawless). Its genius is its demonstration that the sentence "God does not exist" is a self-contradictory sentence. That is why only a fool could utter it.

Take note of how very Platonic Anselm's argument is. First, it is purely **a priori**—that is, it makes no appeal whatsoever to sensorial observation; it appeals exclusively to pure reason. Second, it makes explicit the Platonic view that the "most perfect" equals "the most real." (Recall the Simile of the Line.)

The ontological proof has had a long and checkered history. We shall see it again more than once before our narration ends. Many think that Immanuel Kant finally put it to rest in the eighteenth century (by showing that the flaw in the argument was not one of logic but of <u>grammar</u>); but even today, 900 years after it was written, the argument has astute defenders.

Two problems that plagued the philosophers of the Middle Ages were the PROBLEM OF FAITH vs. REASON, and the PROBLEM OF THE UNIVERSALS. These received their best medieval solution at the hands of Thomas Aquinas in the thirteenth century. The first problem concerned the question of whether to emphasize the claims of divine revelation or the claims of philosophy in one's conception of reality, and there were extremists in both camps. We've seen that philosophers like John Scotus Erigena had purely conceptual schemes in which there seemed to be no room for mere religious belief. Even St. Anselm's God seemed purely philosophical and a far cry from the Stern Father and Vengeful Judge of the Old Testament. On the other end of the spectrum was the antiphilosopher TERTULLIAN (169–220), whose famous cry was, "<u>Credo quia absurdum</u>"—"I believe that which is absurd"—with the implication that he believed it <u>because</u> it was absurd.

The debate between these two groups reached a high pitch and produced a number of startling claims, such as the view of the group called "the Latin Averröists," who, thinking they were following the lead of the great Arab philosopher Averröes, produced the "Doctrine of the Double Truth." This was the view that on many issues there were two mutually contradictory truths, one produced by faith

Credo Quia Absurdum

and one by reason, but both valid from their respective points of view. So, for example, from the anatomical perspective, the human being was a compilation of organs that, when they ceased to function, brought about the termination of the person; but from the theological perspective, the human being was a soul that was, through God's grace, immortal.

This theory, though logically unsatisfactory, did for a short time play the historically positive role of allowing science to develop without having to conceive of itself in theological terms.

The other vexing problem of the day, the "problem of the universals," was the question concerning the status of the referents of words. The problem was introduced into the Middle Ages by Boethius, who had translated from the Greek an essay about Aristotle by the neo-Platonic author

Porphyry (232–304). The latter had queried the ontological status of genera and species. We know that there exist individual things that we call "whales"; but does the genus "Balaenoptera," or the species "Balaenoptera physalis" (fin whale), or the species "Balaenoptera musculus" (blue whale) exist in nature, or are they only artificial categories existing merely in the mind? (The same problem appears in sentences like "This dog is brown." Do the words dog and brown only name the individual or the classes of canines and brown things, and are those classes real or artificial?)

The debate that ensued was, of course, similar to the debate between Plato and Aristotle over the status of the forms, but the original works of the Greeks were lost to the philosophers of the early Middle Ages, and it took them 900 years to arrive at the point that Aristotle had gained in one generation. The issue reached such a state of confusion that John of Salisbury (ca. 1115–ca. 1180) claimed that in his day there were as many ideas on the subject as there were heads. The extremes in this debate were represented, on one side, by the strict Platonists (today called "exaggerated realists"). They held that classes were not only real but <u>more</u> real than individuals. Anselm himself was a representative of this view. The other extreme, represented by ROSCELIN (ca. 1050–1120) and WILLIAM of OCKHAM (ca. 1280–ca. 1349), was the doctrine known as "nominalism" from the Latin word for "name"— <u>nom</u>. According to this view, which was eventually found unacceptable by the Church, only particulars are real, and words denoting classes are <u>merely</u> names. According to the nominalists, the system of names creates differences and similarities, which exist only in the mind of the speaker or in the system of language itself.

You and I may smile when we are told by anthropologists that an Amazonian tribe includes in the same class toads, palm leaves, and arm pits (namely, the class of entities that are warm and dry on top and damp and dark underneath), but the nominalist asks us if this classification is any more arbitrary than our claim that whales and moles are members of the same class (namely, the class of entities with mammary glands)?

As was mentioned earlier, it was THOMAS AQUINAS (1225–1274) who is generally credited with working out the best medieval solution both to the problem of faith vs. reason, and the problem of the universals.

Prima mangiare, poi filosofare!

Thomas was an Italian nobleman who ran away from his family's castle to join the Dominican Order (where, by the way, he was so well fed that a niche eventually had to be carved out of the dinner table to accommodate his ample girth). Before we talk about his philosophy, let's say something about the world he inhabited, thirteenth-century Europe.

More than 100 years had elapsed between Anselm's death and Thomas's birth. In that century, European scholars were becoming more and more acquainted with the "lost" works of the classical age through Christendom's extended contact with the Arab and Jewish philosophers of Moslem Spain. Not only were the works of Aristotle rediscovered, but magnificent commentaries on his philosophy were provided by the Spanish metaphysicians MAIMONIDES (1135–1204), a Jew, and AVERRÖES (1126–1198), an Arab. Though the theories of Aristotle were found to be shocking by some, his philosophy was actually more compatible with the new this-worldly attitude of the thirteenth century than was the now somewhat stale otherworldliness of Platonic thought. The human race had survived the millennium. The year 1000 had passed without the world ending, as many had expected.

The old apocalyptic prophecies faded further into the future, and, as Europe emerged from the darkest moments of the Dark Ages, interest in the world of here and now was revived. Aristotle surfaced as the champion of these new interests. It fell to Thomas Aquinas to "Christianize" him—no easy task considering that Aristotle held such un-Christian views as:

A. The earth is eternal. (There never was a creation.)
B. God is indifferent to human affairs. (He doesn't even know we exist.)
C. The Soul is not immortal.
D. The goal of life is happiness.
E. Pride is a virtue and humility a vice.

No surprise that Aristotle's works were banned by the University of Paris in 1210. (Indeed, Thomas's works themselves were condemned at Paris and at Oxford just after his death.)

Thomas Aquinas wrote over forty volumes. His leading works are two encyclopedic projects, the *Summa theologica* and the *Summa contra gentiles*. These tremendously systematic works comprise a whole structure that has often been compared to the Gothic cathedrals, which were the new architectural style of his day. Like them, Thomas's work is not only a mirror held up to late medieval society but also a beacon unto it.

Thomas's main job was that of <u>reconciliation</u>, not only the reconciliation of Aristotle with Christendom but also that of Reason with Faith and of the warring sides in the debate over the status of universals. Concerning the latter, Thomas was able to take advantage of the Aristotelian solution: Universals are neither autonomous forms nor mere mental states. They are "embedded" in particular objects as their "whatness." The human mind has the power of <u>abstraction</u> based on its ability to recognize real similarities that exist in nature. These abstractions become <u>concepts</u>. This solution came to be known as

MODERATE REALISM. (It had been anticipated 120 years earlier by PETER ABELARD [1079–1142], whose view is called CONCEPTUALISM.)

Concerning the problem of reason vs. faith, Thomas began by distinguishing between <u>philosophy</u> and **theology**. The philosopher uses <u>human</u> <u>reason</u> alone. The theologian accepts <u>revelation</u> as his authority.

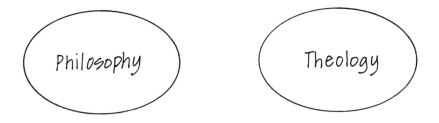

Then Thomas distinguished between REVEALED THEOLOGY (accepted purely on faith) and NATURAL THEOLOGY (susceptible of the proof of reason). That is, he showed where philosophy and theology overlap.

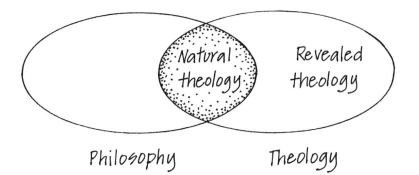

When reason cannot establish the claims of faith, Thomas admitted this and left those claims to the theologians and to personal belief (e.g., the claim that the universe has a beginning in time).

Most of Thomas's system is concerned with natural theology. Typical of this sphere are Thomas's proofs of God's existence. He provided five such proofs. Three of the "five ways" are very similar. We will select the second of the five as representative of Thomas's natural theology:

> In the world of sense we find there is an order of efficient causes. There is no case known (neither is it, indeed, possible) in which a thing is found to be the efficient cause of itself; for so it would be prior to itself, which is impossible. Now in efficient causes it is not possible to go on to infinity. . . . Now to take away the cause is to take away the effect. Therefore if there be no first cause among efficient causes, there will be no ultimate, nor any intermediate cause. . . . Therefore it is necessary to admit a first efficient cause, to which everyone gives the name of God.

In the most superficial reading of his proof, Thomas was giving us a domino theory and simply saying that, if there is a series of causes and effects, such a series must be caused by a being who is itself uncaused, other-

THE BUCK STOPS HERE

wise we will have an infinite regress, which Thomas finds intellectually repugnant. This version of the argument was submitted to careful scrutiny (e.g., by David Hume in the eighteenth century). Thomas's alleged knowledge of an order of causes was challenged, as well as the claim that an infinite series of causes is impossible. However, Thomistic scholars have demonstrated that the "Second Way" is more complicated than it appears to be, involving a horizontal system of causes (in which an infinite series cannot be disproved) and a hierarchical system of dependencies (which, according to Thomas, cannot admit of an infinite regress).

Infinity This Way (Maybe)

Whatever its validity, there are some historically notable features about this and the four other Thomistic proofs. Unlike the ontological proof of Anselm, they all begin with an **a posteriori** claim, that is, with an appeal to observation. This is one of the Aristotelian characteristics of the argument, and in its commitment to the reality of the observable world, it contrasts greatly with the Platonism of Anselm's a priori proof. Still, there are vestiges of Platonism in the "five ways," including whatever appeal there is to a <u>hierarchy</u> of causes.

Like Aristotle's philosophy, all of Thomas's thought is teleological. This is especially true in his ethics. Human activity is viewed as a means–end structure. We choose desired goals, then choose among acts that lead to those goals. The acts are relative to the ends, but the ends (health, beauty, duty) are themselves relative to some absolute ends that give meaning to the relative ends; otherwise, every series of actions would lead to an infinite regress.

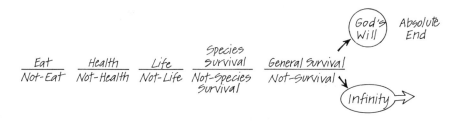

(Notice this is the same kind of argument that led Thomas to posit God as an uncaused cause.) If we want to make correct choices, we must know what the ultimate goal is. Aristotle said it was happiness. Thomas agreed but thought he now knew what the Greeks did not—that happiness itself must be eternal to be an absolute. Our happiness, hence our correct choices and acts, depends on knowledge of God—not just on philosophical knowledge of God but on the expectation of that full and final knowledge, the Beatific Vision.

Thomas himself seems to have experienced some kind of ecstatic realization two years before his death (a pre-figuring of the Beatific Vision?), which caused him to cease writing. He said that in the face of that experience, all his words were like mere straw.

The work of St. Thomas Aquinas represents the apogee of scholastic philosophy. But at the very moment when **scholasticism** was being articulated as the most excellent statement of the high medieval mind, there were already currents developing that would begin to undermine the scholastic synthesis, foreshadowing as they did the birth of a new, more secularly oriented world. These were the voices of men who, intentionally or unintentionally, separated the theological from the philosophical in ways that prepared the path for the "new science" of the Renaissance. Such was the thought of ROGER BACON (ca. 1212–ca. 1292), whose disdain for speculative metaphysics and whose curiosity about the natural world influenced others to move along the new path—people like JOHN DUNS SCOTUS (ca. 1265–ca. 1307), WILLIAM of OCKHAM (ca. 1280–ca. 1349), JOHN BURIDAN (ca. 1300–ca. 1358), and NICHOLAS of ORESME (1320–1382). And these anti-scholastic philosophers prepared the way for a new brand of thinkers in the next two centuries who would be neither theologians nor philosophers, as we have come to know them, but scientists—men like NIKOLAUS COPERNICUS (1473–1543), TYCHO BRAHE (1546–1601), JOHANNES KEPLER (1571–1630), GALILEO GALILEI (1564–1642), and WILLIAM HARVEY (1578–1657). It would be they, along with artists and politicians, and not the metaphysicians who would set the tone of the new age.

V.
THE 17th AND 18th
CENTURIES

   Though there were a number of lesser philosophers during the Renaissance, the first truly magnificent philosophical system of the modern period was that of the Frenchman . . .

RENÉ DESCARTES (1596–1650)

Descartes may not have been very good looking, but he was SMART!

$$Z = X^2 + Y^2$$

Descartes first carved a niche for himself in the pantheon of intellectual giants by discovering ANALYTICAL GEOMETRY, thereby fulfilling the old Pythagorean dream of demonstrating the relation between plane geometry and pure algebra.

Having made his contribution to math, in 1633 Descartes was about to publish his manuscript on physics, but when it dawned on him that seventeen years earlier Galileo Galilei had been arrested by the Inquisition for teaching views about the physical world that were very close to Descartes's own views, Descartes ran, did not walk, to his publisher to withdraw his manuscript.

Galileo's crime had been to peer through his newly invented telescope and discover that the planet Jupiter had four moons.

Why should anybody care? Least of all, why should the Brothers of the Inquisition care?

Because the Renaissance mind had inherited from the medieval world the view that the Garden of Eden was the belly button of the universe and that God had created the rest of the cosmos in concentric layers around the stage of the human drama.

Of course, there had been rumors floating around that the sun and not the earth was the center of the planetary system, but the scientific evidence against that view was the undisputed fact that the moon orbits the earth. If the sun is the center of everything, then why doesn't the moon orbit the sun instead of the earth?

So, if Galileo proved that Jupiter has four moons that orbit it, then he had pulled the last strut out from under the geocentric theory of the universe. As Freud was to say later, this was the first of the three major blows against the human's conception of his own self-importance.

I don't think I can take any more revelations, Doc.

(The other two were Darwin's revelation that we are only animals and Freud's discovery that we are SICK animals.)

It was too much for the Brothers of the Inquisition, so off went Galileo to jail.

Descartes was a good but modern Catholic. He believed the Church had made a big mistake in the Galileo episode. He correctly saw that if religion tried to stem the tide of science, religion would be swept away. But Descartes did not want to have to go to jail to prove it.

So he decided to ease his ideas about physics onto an unsuspecting religious establishment by smuggling them into a book of philosophy, called *Meditations*, which, in a groveling and self-effacing manner, he dedicated to "the Most Wise and Illustrious Doctors of the Sacred Faculty of Theology in Paris."

Meanwhile, to his friend he wrote, ". . . the six Meditations contain all the fundamental ideas of my physics. But please keep this quiet." Descartes hoped that the theologians would be convinced by his arguments before they realized that their own views had been refuted.

In his *Meditations on First Philosophy*, Descartes announced a massive intellectual project. He related his intention to tear down the edifice of knowledge and rebuild it from the foundations up.

To discover a firm foundation of absolute certainty upon which to build his objective system of knowledge, Descartes chose a method of "radical doubt," whose motto was "De omnibus dubitandum,"—everything is to be doubted. So Descartes would doubt away anything that could possibly be doubted, no matter how weak the grounds were for doubting, until he could discover a proposition that was logically indubitable. This proposition, if it existed, would be the absolutely certain foundation of all knowledge.

Descartes began his philosophical journal while sitting at his desk in front of the fire. He wrote, "Everything that I have hitherto accepted his been learned from the senses." But the senses are known deceivers, and it is not prudent ever to trust a known liar.

Descartes's point is clear. We all know about optical illusions (the "bent oar" in the pond, the "water" on the road, the tracks which "meet at the

horizon"), as well as illusions associated with the other senses. So in one fell swoop, radical doubt had deprived Descartes of all sensory information.

But Descartes immediately felt he had gone too far. Only a madman could stare at his hands and wonder if they really were his hands. It seemed that in one step, radical doubt had led not to philosophy but to lunacy.

But then Descartes recalled that on other occasions he had believed he was sitting before the fire, looking at his hands, only to awaken later to discover that it all was a dream. Much to his amazement, Descartes realized that there is no test to prove with absolute certainty that at any given moment one is not dreaming. (Any test you can <u>think</u>, you can <u>dream</u>, so it's no test at all.)

Therefore, consistent with radical doubt, Descartes assumed that it was always possible that he <u>was</u> dreaming. This totally undermined the possibility that the senses could provide us with certain knowledge.

What about mathematics? Perhaps it can be a candidate for absolute certainty. Descartes said, "Whether I am asleep or awake, 2 and 3 are 5, and a square has no more than four sides." But radical doubt required Descartes to suspect even the simplest propositions of arithmetic if there was <u>any</u> reason for doing so. Well, what if the Creator of the universe

was not the benevolent God of Catholicism, but an Evil Genius, a malevolent demon whose sole purpose was that of deception, . . . so that even the most simple mathematical judgment would always be false? Could Descartes know for sure that such a demon did not exist?

No! There existed the logical possibility that Descartes's mind was being controlled externally by a malevolent force. So Descartes assumed that all the world was nothing but the dream of the Evil Genius. Descartes asked, under these conditions could <u>anything</u> be certain?

Descartes concluded that there was one and only one thing that was absolutely certain—that he existed! His assertion, "I THINK, THEREFORE I AM," was true whether he was dreaming, whether the senses deceived, and whether there was an Evil Genius. It was, in fact, <u>necessarily</u> true. It could not be denied or even doubted without self-contradiction. (Try it! If you say "I doubt that I exist" haven't you in fact proved that you do exist?)

Having discovered certainty in selfhood and having established that his self was his consciousness (for it is possible to doubt that you have a body, but it is impossible to doubt that you have a mind; therefore, your self and your mind must be identical), Descartes must now find a way of escaping the confines of his own subjctivity and establishing the existence of an external world. To do so, he analyzed the contents of his mind and discovered it contained certain innate ideas (shades of Plato), including these:

"SELF"
"IDENTITY"
"SUBSTANCE"
"GOD"

Using a version of St. Anselm's **"ontological argument"** (remember, it was a priori, making no appeal to the external world—

a world that for Descartes did not yet exist), he "proved" God's existence, thereby disposing of the Evil Genius. (A perfect, omnipotent, omnibenevolent God would not allow such a Deceiver to exist.)

Thereby, Descartes recovered math into his system (the only objection to math had been the Evil Genius hypothesis). By applying math to his innate idea of corporeal substance, Descartes came up with what he took to be the correct account of reality—the world as known by mathematical physics. Descartes had pulled it off. He showed that you can have both God and Galileo!

However, Descartes did leave himself with a few problems. First, he had replaced the commonsense view of the relation between self and world (what philosophers call "naive realism") . . . but he replaced it with a most circuitous route, indeed. Second, he assigned all perceivable qualities ("red," "blue," "sweet," "warm," "melodious") to the mind and left only mathematically measurable quantities in the external world—a cold, colorless, odorless, soundless, tasteless world of matter in motion.

NAIVE REALISM
"What you see is what you get."

CARTESIAN REALISM
"What you see is not what you get."

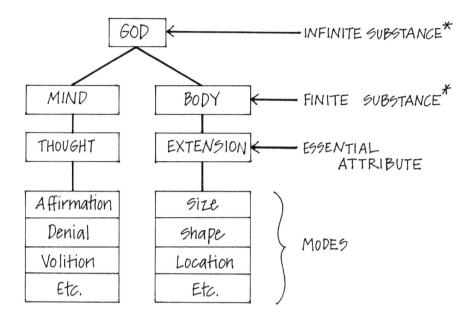

*SUBSTANCE is defined as "an existent thing that requires nothing but itself in order to exist."

Furthermore, Descartes's picture of the world was hopelessly divided into substances that were defined in ways that mutually excluded each other. How could the mental world (a nonspatial, purely spiritual sphere) have any effect on the physical world of crass matter, and vice-versa, in this radically dualistic scheme of things? Descartes tried to solve the problem by claiming that MIND meets BODY at the center of the brain, in the pineal gland. (It should have been obvious that this solution would not work.)

No matter WHERE mind meets body, at that place it becomes body, since it then has location, which is a mode of physical substance. At this point, Descartes conveniently died of the common cold while visiting his benefactress, Queen Christina of Sweden, in order to explain to her the function of the pineal gland. Thereby, he left to his followers the legacy of his radical dualism.

Meanwhile, across the channel, THOMAS HOBBES (1588–1679) was dealing with problems similar to those addressed by his contemporary René Descartes. Hobbes was a contentious old codger who dabbled in everything. (His experiments in math led him to claim that he had squared the circle and cubed the sphere.) At one point or another he managed to antagonize every political party in Britain and had to flee to France.

Thomas Hobbes Squares the Circle

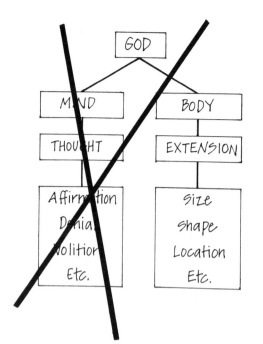

Hobbes solved Descartes's dualistic dilemma simply by dismantling dualism. He loudly proclaimed a form of mechanistic materialism reminiscent of Democritus's atomism, thereby rejecting one side of Descartes's diagram; and Hobbes's thinly disguised atheism rejected Descartes's "infinite substance" as well. For Hobbes, the only things that existed in reality were bodies in motion. Despite his claim that "there exist everywhere only bodies," Hobbes did not actually deny the existence of thoughts. He simply held them to be "phantasms," shadows of brain activity, mere epiphenomena that had no practical effect on the physical system. Similarly, though he was a determinist, he was, like the stoics and St. Augustine, a "soft determinist." (A soft determinist believes that freedom and determinism are compatible.) It was OK to talk about freedom as long as all one meant by it was "unimpeded movement." (Water flows down a channel both necessarily and freely.)

Hobbes's psychology is very pessimistic. Every living organism obeys laws of individual survival; therefore, all human acts are motivated by self-interest and the quest for power. Altruism is not just a bad idea; it is impossible. Far from being immoral, <u>egoism</u> is the only show in town. . . . "Of the voluntary acts of every man, the object is some good to himself."

Hobbes is best known for his political philosophy, which is influenced by his egoistic theory of motivation. He recognized the state as an artificial monster ("the Leviathan"), which restricts what little freedom there is in nature and flaunts its power over the individual, but Hobbes justified the existence of the political state by contrasting it to the notorious "state of nature," dominated by scarcity and fear, where "every man is enemy to every man," and where life is "solitary, poor, nasty, brutish and short." In the state of nature, there is no law, no morality, no property, and only one "natural right"—the right to protect oneself using any means at one's disposal, including violence and slaughter. If two people are on a desert island and there isn't an abundance of coconuts to eat, then neither dares turn his back nor sleep lest the other bash him with a rock in order to get all the coconuts for himself. However, if both are rational, they will realize that the most likely way of surviving is to agree with each other to forswear violence and share the coconuts. The trouble is, given the selfish nature that Hobbes attributes to all of us, there is no reason at all for either party to keep the agreement if they can figure a way to break it with impunity. So there is every reason for them to distrust each other. Despite their "agreement," neither dares yet to sleep a wink. The solution requires that a third party be found. The first two parties give to the third party all the rocks (and perhaps an army), and they give up their right to violence. In exchange, she promises to use her absolute power to guarantee that the first two parties honor their agreement with each other. ("She" may be either a monarch or a parliament—in either case she is the source of all authority.)

The Sovereign

This is Hobbes's famous "social contract." He realized that there is nothing to prevent the new sovereign from abusing her power (indeed, given <u>her</u> egoistic nature and innate lust for power, it is almost inevitable that she would do so), but he believed that the State, even with its necessary abuse of power, was better than the alternative—the horrors of anarchy in "the state of nature."

(It should be mentioned that, typically, Hobbes's political theory managed to please no one in Britain. The parliamentarians didn't like it because of its absolutist implications, and the king didn't like it because of its denial of the divine right of monarchs.)

« »

Back on the continent, the Dutch-born Jewish philosopher BARUCH SPINOZA (1634–1677) was trying to resolve the dilemmas of Descartes's legacy while remaining within the rationalistic tradition that Descartes exemplified. (Rationalists believe that the true source of knowledge is reason, not the senses, and that the correct philosophical model must be an a priori one, not one based

Baruch Spinoza

on empirical generalizations.) Spinoza was, according to Bertrand Russell, "the noblest and most lovable of the great philosophers." This is because he, more than any other philosopher, lived his philosophy, even though he realized that doing so would result in his alienation from both the Jewish and the Christian community alike. Spinoza accepted his excommunication from synagogue, church, and society without rancor, and he never sought fame nor riches, nor even a professorship, living out his life philosophizing and grinding lenses to earn a meager living. He accepted as his reward the state of tranquility afforded to him by his philosophy, and his motto could well have been his own epigram, "All excellent things are as difficult as they are rare."

Spinoza tried to submit **Cartesian** metaphysics to a geometric method even more rigorous than that used by Descartes himself. Like Descartes's, Spinoza's philosophy is centered on a definition of SUBSTANCE, but Spinoza had detected a contradiction in Descartes's account. Descartes had said, "By substance we can conceive nothing else than a thing which exists in such a way as to stand in need of nothing beyond itself." Then Descartes had gone on to say, "And in truth, there can be conceived but one substance which is absolutely independent, and that is God," which he called "infinite substance." Despite this admission that by definition there could exist only one kind of being that was absolutely independent, Descartes (in a contradictory manner, according to Spinoza) proceeded to distinguish between "infinite substance" and "finite substances"—the latter were called corporeal substance (body) and mental substance (mind). This radical dualism led Descartes to his notorious mind/body problem and his universally scorned pineal gland solution.

Spinoza avoided this embarrassment by accepting Descartes's definition of substance (as that which is absolutely independent) and taking deadly seriously the inference that there could be only ONE such substance. (If there were two, they would limit each other's independence.)

Furthermore, because finiteness would constitute a limitation on God's absolute independence, Spinoza defined God as having infinite attributes. So once again, one arrives at the conclusion that there can be but one substance because any substance other than God would have to possess attributes that have already been defined as belonging to God.

Let's look at a schematized comparison of the systems of Descartes and Spinoza:

*(An <u>attribute</u>, for Descartes, is a characteristic that is the <u>essence</u> of a substance [i.e., that which is essential to it]. For Spinoza, an attribute is a characteristic that to the human intellect <u>seems</u> to be an essence. A <u>mode</u> is a specific modification of an attribute [i.e., a characteristic of a characteristic].)

Like Descartes, Spinoza equated "infinite substance" with God, but he also equated it with "Nature." The equation "Nature = God" makes him a pantheist. (It is also this equation that got him into trouble with both the Jewish and Christian theologians.) There are two human perspectives on reality (i.e., on God): one viewed through the attribute of mind (resulting in IDEALISM, the claim that only mind exists) and one viewed through the attribute of body (resulting in MATERIALISM, the view that only matter exists). In theory, there is an indefinite number of other perspectives on reality, but only these two are open to the human intellect. A completely consistent idealistic or materialistic account of reality can be given, but no consistent dualism is possible. Dualism involves a confusion of perspectives. (So much for Descartes's pineal gland.)

The true philosopher attempts to transcend the purely human perspective and view reality <u>sub</u> <u>specie</u> <u>aeternitatis</u>, that is, from the perspective of reality itself. From this perspective, one comes to realize that the human has no privileged position in the cosmos, the human has no more and no less dignity than anything else in nature. One must come to love everything, which is to say, to love God (because one must either love everything, or nothing at all). The <u>love</u> <u>of</u> <u>God</u> is tantamount to the <u>knowledge</u> <u>of</u> <u>God</u>, which is to say, a philosophical knowledge of reality. This difficult intellectual love of God is, like that of Platonism, a form of rationalism tainted with **mysticism**. It

The Unrequited Love of Nature

also contains a stoic component, insofar as knowledge of reality leads one to realize that everything that happens, happens of necessity. There is no **randomness** and no freedom of the will. But the realization that there is no such thing as free will, neither for God nor for humans, can itself be a liberating realization because one is thereby freed from the demands of desire and passion, both of which were seen by Spinoza as murky emotions that manage to control us only because of our failure to grasp the rational structure of reality. With knowledge, these emotions can be transformed into clear and distinct ideas leading to a kind of blessedness and joy. Spinoza wrote: "There cannot be too much joy: it is always good: but melancholy is always bad."

« »

The third of the great Continental rationalists was the German GOTTFRIED LEIBNIZ (1646–1716). He was a universal genius who made significant advances in symbolic logic

Gottfried Leibniz

"Leibniz was one of the supreme intellects of all time, but as a human being he was not admirable."

Bertrand Russell

and who created a plan for the invasion of Egypt, which may have been used by Napoleon 120 years later. He also invented a calculating machine that could add, subtract, and do square roots. Furthermore, he discovered infinitesimal calculus simultaneously with Sir Isaac Newton (and got into a squabble with him concerning who had stolen the idea from whom).

Like Spinoza, Leibniz wished to correct the errors of Cartesian metaphysics without rejecting its main structure; but Leibniz was not satisfied with Spinoza's pantheistic monism nor with his naturalism (i.e., his view that all is nature and that the human being has no special status in reality). Leibniz wanted a return to a Cartesian system with real individuals and a transcendent God. Leibniz's system, as set forth in his *Monadology* and *Essays in Theodicy*, can be summarized in terms of three principles:

"the **principle of identity**," "the principle of sufficient reason," and "the principle of internal harmony."

1. The PRINCIPLE OF IDENTITY: Leibniz divided all propositions into two types, which later philosophers would call ANALYTIC propositions and SYNTHETIC propositions. Take a look at the following table:

ANALYTIC	SYNTHETIC
A. TRUE BY DEFINITION: (true merely by virtue of the meanings of the words in the sentences.) B. NECESSARY: (their opposites are self-contradictions. They <u>cannot</u> be false.) C. A PRIORI: (their truth is known independently of observation.)	A. NOT TRUE BY DEFINITION: (their truth or falsity depends not on <u>meanings</u> but on facts in the world.) B. NOT NECESSARY, RATHER CONTINGENT: (<u>could</u> be false if facts were different.) C. A POSTERIORI: (their truth or falsity is known by observation.)

Following are some examples of <u>analytic</u> <u>sentences</u>:

A. "All bachelors are men."

B. "2 + 3 = 5"

C. "Either A or not—A"

This category includes definitions and parts of definitions (A) and arithmetic and the principles of logic [(B) and (C)]. These were said by Leibniz to be based on the principle of identity in the sense that this principle is the positive counterpart of the **principle of noncontradiction** (which says that it cannot be the case that A and not—A at the same time) in that the negation of every analytic

159

sentence is a self-contradiction. (E.g., "<u>Not</u> all bachelors are men" implies the contradictory assertion, "Some men are not men" [because the definition of "bachelor" is "unmarried man"].)

Following are some examples of <u>synthetic</u> <u>sentences</u>:

A. "The cat is on the mat."

B. "Caesar crossed the Rubicon in 49 B.C."

Now, having drawn what many philosophers believe to be a very important distinction, Leibniz made the surprising move of claiming that all synthetic sentences are really analytic. <u>Sub</u> <u>specie</u> <u>aeternitatis</u>, that is to say, from God's point of view, it is the case that all true sentences are <u>necessarily</u> true, even though it doesn't seem to be the case to us humans. For Leibniz, Tuffy the cat's characteristic of "being on the mat at time T¹" is a characteristic necessary to that specific cat in the same way that "being a feline" is necessary to it.

You see, I couldn't <u>not</u> be on the mat!

160

2. This brings us to the PRINCIPLE OF SUFFICIENT REASON. According to Leibniz, for anything that exists, there is some reason <u>why</u> it exists and why it exists exactly as it does exist. Leibniz claimed that this is the main principle of rationality and that anyone who rejects this principle is irrational. If the cat is on the mat, then there must be some reason why the cat exists at all, and why it is on the mat and not, for example, in the dishwasher. Both of these reasons should be open to human scientific inquiry, though perhaps only God can know why the cat exists <u>necessarily</u> and is necessarily on the mat.

What is true of the cat is true of the whole cosmos, said Leibniz. There must be a reason why the universe exists at all, and this reason ought to be open to rational human inquiry. Leibniz asked, "Why is there something rather than nothing?" Like St. Thomas, he concluded that the only possible answer would be in terms of an uncaused cause, an all-perfect God whose being was itself necessary. So if Leibniz was right, we can derive the proof of the existence of God from the bare notion of rationality.

3. Which takes us to the PRINCIPLE OF INTERNAL HARMONY. If there is a God, God must be both rational and good. Such a divinity, Leibniz told us, must desire and be capable of creating the maximum amount of existence possible ("metaphysical perfection") and the maximum amount of activity possible ("moral perfection"). Therefore, at the moment of creation, God entertained all possibilities. He actualized only those possibilities that would guarantee the maximum amount of metaphysical and moral perfection. For example, God not only considered the individual "Caesar" in all of Caesar's ramifications (would

write *The Gallic Wars,* would cross the Rubicon in 49 B.C., would die on the Ides of March) before actualizing him. Perhaps he considered actualizing (i.e., creating) "Gaesar" and "Creasar" in Caesar's place, who, as potential actualizations, were identical to Caesar in all respects except that Gaesar would cross <u>not</u> the Rubicon but the Delaware River in 49 B.C., and Creasar would cross the Love Canal. God saw that <u>only</u> Caesar was compatible with the rest of the possibilities that he would activate, and therefore he actualized him and not the others. A similar thought experiment could be performed with God's creation of BRUTUS (as opposed, perhaps, to "Brautus" and "Brutos"). So the relation between Caesar and Brutus is not a causal one but one of <u>internal</u> <u>harmony</u>. And the same holds true of the relations among all substances. God activates only substances that will necessarily harmonize with each other to the greatest extent possible. This now explains why all true sentences are analytic. If Tuffy is on the mat at 8 P.M., that is because <u>this</u> cat <u>must</u> be on the mat at 8 P.M. (otherwise it is not Tuffy, but another cat). It also explains Leibniz's notorious claim that "this is the best of all possible worlds." The world may appear very imperfect to <u>you,</u> but if you knew what the alternative was, you would be very grateful indeed to God. (It is this feature of Leibniz's philosophy that was to be lampooned by Voltaire in *Candide.*)

Every philosopher in the 250-year period after the publication of Descartes's *Meditations* conceived of reality in terms of SUBSTANCES. Leibniz called these substances MONADS, which he defined as "units of psychic force." They are simple (i.e., they have no parts), and each is "pregnant" with all of its future states. Each monad is a mirror of the

Candide Inspects the Ruins of Lisbon After the Earthquake of 1755

entire universe (God actualized only those monads that
<u>would</u> mirror the rest of the universe), but they perceive
the rest of reality only as features of their own inner
states. "The monads have no windows." All monads have a
psychic life, but some have a higher degree of psychic life
than others. These monads (or communities of monads
clustered around a "dominant monad") are conscious.

Some conscious clusters of monads are also free, and these are human beings. (Of course, as in the theory of St. Augustine, God already knows how they will spend their freedom.)

The view's lousy, but they've got great video!

Perhaps it can be said that Leibniz's philosophy solves the problems of Descartes's dualism, but it does so at the expense of common sense and seems to be fraught with as many problems as Descartes's theory. It should come as no surprise that a philosopher would soon rise to the defense of common sense and of observation, reacting against the speculative flights of fancy of a Spinoza or a Leibniz. Such a philosopher was John Locke.

After a Philosophy Lecture, Three Students Actually Find a Monad Behind a Pile of Old Socks

JOHN LOCKE (1632–1704) was the first of the classical British empiricists. (Empiricists believed that all knowledge derives from experience. These philosophers were hostile to rationalistic metaphysics, particularly to its unbridled use of speculation, its grandiose claims, and its epistemology grounded in innate ideas.) In his *Essay Concerning Human Understanding*, Locke began his attack on Descartes's "innate ideas" by threatening them with Occam's Razor. ("Occam's Razor" is a principle of simplification derived from William of Ockham, or Occam. It cautions, "Do

John Locke

not multiply entitles beyond necessity." Given two theories, each of which adequately accounts for all the observable data, the simpler theory is the correct theory.) If Locke could account for all human knowledge without making reference to innate ideas, then his theory would be simpler, hence better, than that of Descartes. He wrote, "Let us then suppose the mind to be, as we say, white paper, void of all characters, without any ideas: How comes it to be furnished? To this I answer, in one word, from EXPERIENCE."

"principle of plentitude"

So the mind at birth is a <u>tabula rasa</u>, a blank slate, and is informed only by "experience," that is, by sense experience and acts of reflection. Locke built from this an epistemology beginning with a pair of distinctions: one between SIMPLE and COMPLEX ideas and another between PRIMARY and SECONDARY qualities.

The <u>Tabula Rasa</u> Being Marked by Experience

Simple ideas originate in any one sense (though some of them, like "motion," can derive either from the sense of sight or the sense of touch). These ideas are "simple" in the sense that they cannot be further broken down into yet simpler entities. (If a person does not understand the idea of "yellow," you can't explain it to him. All you can do is point to a sample and say, "yellow.") These simple ideas are Locke's primary data, his psychological atoms. All knowledge is in one way or another built up out of them.

"Complex ideas" are, for example, combinations of simple ideas. These result in our knowledge of particular things (e.g., "an apple"—derived from the simple ideas "red-spherical-sweet"), comparisons ("darker than"), relations ("north of"), and abstractions ("gratitude"). Even abstractions, or "general ideas," are nevertheless <u>particular</u> ideas that stand for collections. (This doctrine places Locke close to the theory known in the medieval world as "nominalism." All

The Problem: To Construct Knowledge from Simple Ideas

the empiricists share with the nominalists the anti-Platonic thesis that <u>only particulars exist</u>.)

Locke's distinction between "primary" and "secondary" qualities is one that he borrowed from Descartes and Galileo, who had in turn borrowed them from Democritus. Primary qualities are characteristics of external objects. These qualities really do inhere in those objects. (Extension, size, shape, and location are examples of primary qualities.) Secondary qualities are characteristics that we often attribute to external objects, but that in fact exist only in the mind, yet are <u>caused</u> by real features of external objects. (Examples of secondary qualities are colors, sounds, and tastes.) This view of the mind has come to be known as REPRESENTATIVE REALISM. According to it, the mind represents the external world but it does not duplicate it. (The view that the mind literally duplicates external reality is called "naive realism.") The mind is something like a photograph in that there are features of a photo that very accurately represent the world (e.g., a good picture of three people correctly depicts the fact that there are three people and that each of them has two eyes, one nose, and one mouth), and there are features of the photograph that belong exclusively to the photo (its glossiness, its two-dimensionality, the white border around its content). So, as in Descartes's system, there is a real world out there, and it has certain real qualities—the primary qualities. Now, these qualities—what are they qualities of? In answering this question, Locke never abandoned the basic Cartesian metaphysics of substance.

A real quality must be a quality of a real thing, and real things are substances. (Once again, given anything in the world, it is either a substance or a characteristic of a substance.) Well then, what is the status of this pivotal

What Appears to Be Out There   **What Is Out There**

idea of "substance" in Locke's theory? Recall that Descartes had claimed that one could not derive the idea of substance from observation precisely because perception could only generate qualities. For this very reason, it was necessary to posit the idea of substance as an <u>innate idea</u>. But Locke was committed to the rejection of innate ideas and to the claim that all knowledge comes in through the senses. So what did he say about the idea of substance? Rather amazingly, he said the following:

> So that if anyone will examine himself concerning his notion of pure substance in general, he will find he has no other idea of it at all, but only a supposition of he knows not what <u>support</u> of such qualities which are capable of pro-ducing simple ideas in us.

So, having claimed that he could account for all knowledge purely in terms of "experience" and having arrived at the concept that had dominated philosophy for the last several generations, Locke proclaimed it a mystery and even joked about it. (He compared the philosopher trying to explain substance to the Indian who explained that the world was supported by a great elephant, which in turn was supported by a tortoise, which in turn was supported by—"something, he knew not what.") This is a bit embarrassing, and it is either a rather inauspicious beginning for empiricism or the beginning of the end of the metaphysics of substance. (We will soon see that it is the latter.)

John Locke concerned himself not only with epistemology but with politics as well. In his theory, developed in *Two Treatises on Government*, Locke, like Hobbes, drew a distinction between "the state of nature" and "the political state." However, what he meant by "state of nature" was very different indeed from what Hobbes meant by it. Far from being a condition in which there is "no justice nor injustice, no right nor wrong, no mine and thine distinct," Locke's "state of nature" is a <u>moral</u> state—the state into which we are all born as humans, where we are all bestowed with certain <u>God-given</u> natural rights, the right to "life, health, liberty and possessions." Recall that for Hobbes, there was only one natural right, the right to try to pre-

The State of Nature According to Hobbes

The State of Nature According to Locke

serve one's life. Hobbes seems to have believed that a kind of instinct for survival authorized that right. Locke's theory contains several natural rights, all of which are moral rather than instinctual, and they derive their authority from God. Hobbes purposely left God out of his theory because he was trying to escape medievalism, where all philosophy presupposed God's existence. Hobbes was particularly insistent that there was no such thing as a "natural right to property," since in nature there is no property only possession (". . . only that to be every man's, that he can get; and for so long as he can keep it"). Locke, to the contrary, claimed we have a natural right to whatever part of nature we have "mixed our labor with." So if I till the soil, or cut down a tree and make a house from it, then this garden and that house are <u>mine</u> (and will be my children's when they inherit them from me). Locke did put qualifications on this natural right to property. One can accumulate as much "natural property" as one can use, as long as:

A. it does not spoil in its accumulation.
B. enough has been left for others.
C. its accumulation is not harmful to others.

Locke's wealthy friends were probably glad to hear that "gold and silver may be hoarded up without injury to anyone."

(It is noteworthy that Locke's theory presupposes a state of abundance in nature, whereas Hobbes's presupposes a state of scarcity. It may be true that human nature would express itself very differently in these vastly dissimilar "states of nature.")

According to Locke, individual political states are to be evaluated in terms of how well they protect the natural rights of the individuals living in those states. A good state is one that guarantees and maximizes those rights; a bad state is one that does not guarantee them; and an evil state is one that itself assaults the natural rights. Locke's version of "the social contract" is that all citizens consent to be ruled by a government elected by a majority for just as long as that government protects the natural rights. But a tyrannical government is illegitimate and <u>ought</u> to be revolted against. Note that, unlike Hobbes, Locke is able to distinguish between a legitimate and an illegitimate government and provides a theory of justifiable revolution. It is clear that the "Founding Fathers" used Locke's theory to justify the American revolution, and they incorporated his ideas into our Declaration of Independence and Constitution. Perhaps what is best in the American system derives from what is best in Locke's theory, and some social critics claim that what is worst in the American system is derived from what is worst in Locke's theory. America can be seen as a great Lockean experiment.

George Berkeley

The second of the British empiricists was the Irishman, GEORGE BERKELEY (1685–1753), a teacher at Trinity College in Dublin who eventually became the Anglican Bishop of Cloyne. As a philosopher, he was very impressed by Locke's work and wanted to correct what he took to be its errors and inconsistencies while remaining true to the basic platform of empiricism ("blank slate" theory, **psychological atomism**, nominalism, commitment to Occam's

Razor). In fact, he applied Occam's Razor to the idea of material substance so scrupulously that he shaved it clean away and was left with a type of SUBJECTIVE IDEALISM—the view that only minds and ideas exist.

Early in his *Principles of Human Knowledge*, Berkeley attacked Locke's distinction between primary and secondary qualities. Recall that the former were said to inhere in material substance that existed independently of the mind, whereas the latter existed only in the mind (or, as Berkeley put it, their _esse_ is _percipi_—their "being" is "to be perceived"). Now, Berkeley pointed out that our only access to so-called primary qualities is through secondary qualities. The only way we can know the size, shape, location, or dimensionality of an object is by feeling it or seeing it (i.e., through the secondary qualities of tactile or visual sensation). Berkeley concluded from this that descriptions of "primary qualities" are really only interpretations of secondary qualities—different ways of talking about colors, sounds, tastes, odors, and tactile sensations. Therefore, "primary qualities" too exist only in the mind. Their _esse_ is also _percipi_.

To explain how this translation of secondary qualities into primary qualities was possible, Berkeley drew a distinction between DIRECT PERCEPTION and INDIRECT PERCEPTION. Direct (or "immediate") perception is the passive reception of basic **sense data** (Locke's "secondary qualities" and "simple ideas"). Indirect (or "mediate") perception is the _interpretation_ of those sense data. Consider the process of learning to read. The small child confronts a written page and sees only black "squigglies" on a white background.

(This is direct perception.) Through a process of accul-
turation, the child eventually learns to see these markings
as words, loaded with meanings. (This is indirect perception.) It is an interesting fact that once we've learned to
read, it is very difficult to recover the child's "innocent eye"
and see the words again as mere "squigglies." This
explained to Berkeley why we adults perceive the world as
groupings of THINGS rather than as sense data.
Nevertheless, claimed Berkeley, the "things" we see in the
so-called external world are really only "collections of
ideas," philosophically analyzable into their component
sense data. Said Berkeley,

> As several of these [sense data] are observed to accom-
> pany each other, they come to be marked by one name, and
> so to be reputed as one <u>thing</u>. Thus, for example, a certain
> color, taste, smell, figure and consistence having been
> observed to go together, are accounted one distinct thing,
> signified by the name apple; other collections of ideas con-
> stitute a stone, a tree, a book, and the like sensible things.

What's true of the component parts of a stone is true
of the whole stone. Its <u>esse</u> is also <u>percipi</u>.

Notice that the notion of "material substance" (Locke's "something, I know not what") has simply disappeared in Berkeley's system. And the role played by the rationalists' "innate idea of substance" in explaining how we come to know the world as a concatenation of individual physical objects has been taken over by LANGUAGE. We teach our children <u>words</u>, which organize the ideas in their minds into "things." Berkeley's subjective idealism holds that each of us lives in his or her own subjective world composed of the sense data of the five senses. This is the same world we entered into as infants. But we were taught a language, which is to say, taught to "read" our sense data.

Language is also the cement of INTERSUBJECTIVITY. I am able to bridge the gap between my private world and yours through the shared use of conventional symbols. Without language I would be stuck **solipsistically** in the echo chamber of my own mind. Berkeley believed that with these two categories (sense data and language) he could account for all possible human knowledge—all except the knowledge of GOD. (Berkeley was a bishop, after all, so don't be

When I said that ESSE IS PERCIPI, of course I didn't mean that <u>YOURS</u> was!

surprised to find God playing a key role in Berkeley's philosophy, even if it was a bit embarrassing to him that God's <u>esse</u> is not <u>percipi</u>.) God's existence can be deduced from the regularity and predictability of sense data. If the so-called physical world's "being" is to "be perceived," and hence is dependent on the mind, then why is it that when I return to an empty room that I had vacated earlier, everything is just as I left it? Why didn't the room disappear when I stopped perceiving it? Because God was perceiving it while I was out. God is the guarantor of the laws of

Why Doesn't the Room Disappear When We Leave It?

nature. When it says in the Bible that God created the world, that means that he created sense data and minds (spirits, selves) to perceive them. God did <u>not</u> cause there to be some unperceivable, mysterious stuff—"material substance"—which in turn causes ideas. Believing that there was such a "stuff" was the error of Locke's representative realism. Locke failed to see that the representation <u>is</u> the reality. Berkeley has merely eliminated the "middle man." His theory explains everything that Locke's does but is more economical; hence, according to Occam's Razor, it is <u>better</u> than Locke's. So Berkeley believed.

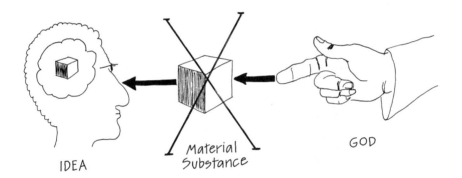

IDEA　　　Material Substance　　　GOD

Berkeley Eliminates the Middle Man

The third of the "Holy Trinity" of British empiricism is the Scot DAVID HUME (1711–1776). He published his first book, *A Treatise of Human Nature*, when he was twenty-seven and he hoped to achieve fame and fortune from it, but, by his own reckoning, it "fell dead-born from the press." Ten years later he rewrote it and published it as *An Enquiry Concerning the Human Understanding*.

David Hume

This book was considerably more successful than its predecessor, possibly because it was a bit more moderate. Today Hume is recognized as the most acute, if the most perplexing, of the British empiricists.

Hume's philosophy began with a revival of Leibniz's analytic/synthetic distinction, or, in Hume's words, a distinction between "relations of ideas" and "matters of fact." It will be recalled that analytic **propositions** are expressed by sentences

A. whose negation leads to a self-contradiction,
B. that are a priori,
C. that are true by definition, and therefore
D. are necessarily true.

Synthetic propositions are expressed by sentences that are the opposite of sentences expressing analytic propositions; that is, they are sentences

A. whose negation does <u>not</u> lead to a self-contradiction,
B. that are a posteriori,
C. that are <u>not</u> true by definition, and
D. when they are true, they are not <u>necessarily</u> true (they <u>can</u> be false).

Now, in accepting this distinction, Hume was admitting that there are such things as <u>a priori necessary truths</u>. It would seem that any empiricist who accepted this was jeopardizing the program of empiricism by recognizing the legitimacy of the rationalists' dream, but Hume defused this situation by adding one more characteristic to the list of features of "relations of ideas." He said that they are all <u>TAUTOLOGICAL</u>, that is, they are all redundant, repetitive, merely verbal truths that provide no new information about the world, only information about the meaning of words. Thus, given the conventions of the English language, it is certainly true that "all sisters are siblings," but saying this tells one nothing about any particular sister that wasn't already known by calling her a sister in the first place. Similarly, anybody who really understands the concept "five" and the concepts "three," "two," and "plus" already knows that "3 + 2 = 5." So the rationalistic dream of a complete description of reality which is a priori and necessarily true is a will-o'-the-wisp because a priori truths aren't descriptions of <u>anything,</u> according to Hume. Only synthetic claims—"matters of fact"—can correctly describe reality, and these claims are necessarily a posteriori. Therefore, all true knowledge about the world must be based on observation. This is, of course, the central thesis of all empiricism.

What Hume was claiming was that there are basically only three categories of analysis. Given any proposition whatsoever, that proposition is either ANALYTIC, SYNTHETIC, or NONSENSE. Hume said:

"When we run over libraries, persuaded of these principles, what havoc must we make? If we take in our hand any volume—of divinity or school metaphysics, for instance—let us ask, <u>Does</u> <u>it</u> <u>contain</u> <u>any</u> <u>abstract</u> <u>reasoning</u> <u>concerning</u> <u>quantity</u> <u>or</u> <u>number</u> [i.e., analytical truths]? No. <u>Does</u> <u>it</u> <u>contain</u> <u>any</u> <u>experimental</u> <u>reasoning</u> <u>concerning</u> <u>matter</u> <u>of</u> <u>fact</u> <u>and</u> <u>existence</u> [i.e., synthetic truths]? No. Commit it then to the flames, for it can contain nothing but sophistry and illusion."

(No wonder Hume lost his job as a librarian.)

David Hume—Librarian

There is, then, very clearly a "Humean method" of philosophizing. One takes any claim which one would like to test, and asks a series of questions about that claim:

1. <u>Is it analytic?</u>

   (This is determined by negating the sentence in which the claim is expressed. If the resultant negative sentence is a self-contradiction, then the original sentence is analytic.)

   ☐ YES (If the answer is YES, the claim is <u>true</u>, but philosophically trivial.)

   ☐ NO (If the answer is NO, go to the next question.)

2. <u>Is it synthetic?</u>

   This question is posed by Hume in the following way: "When we entertain . . . any suspicion that a philosophical term is employed without any meaning or idea (as is but too frequent), we need but inquire, <u>from</u> <u>what</u> <u>impression</u> <u>is</u> <u>that</u> <u>supposed</u> <u>idea</u> <u>derived</u>? And if it be impossible to assign any, this will serve to confirm our suspicion."

In other words, question 2 can be answered affirmatively only if it is possible to trace its ideas back to sense data ("impressions"). For

example, all the ideas in the sentence "This stone is heavy" can be traced back to sense data, hence it passes the empirical criterion of meaning.

☑ YES

But what if, in a particular case, the answer to question 2 is negative?

☑ NO

That is, what if a particular idea cannot be traced to a sense impression? In that case, according to Hume, we must be dealing with vacuous ideas, that is to say, with <u>nonsense</u>.

Now, with Hume's method in hand, if we turn to some of the traditional philosophical topics, like GOD, WORLD, and SELF, we arrive at some pretty startling conclusions. Let's start with the sentence "God exists."

1. Is this proposition analytic?

That is to ask, is its negation ("God does not exist") a self-contradiction? Most people would answer no. Of course, there are some who would answer yes—namely, all those defenders of the "ontological proof of God's existence" (e.g., Anselm, Descartes, Spinoza), but Hume would respond to them by saying that if the sentence "God exists" is analytic, then it is tautological and tells us nothing about reality. The true sentence "A necessary being necessarily exists" still doesn't tell us whether there is a necessary being.

☑ NO

So if we assume that "God exists" is not analytic, the next question is,

2. Is this proposition synthetic?

Hume believed it was impossible to trace the idea of God back to sense data. He said, "Our ideas reach no further than our experience. We have no experience of divine attributes and operations. I need not conclude my syllogism. You can draw the inference yourself." So, although Hume didn't actually say so, his method seems to imply that the idea of God is vacuous and that statements about God are literally non<u>sense</u>.

So much for God in Hume's system. What about the world? Berkeley, using Occam's Razor, had already eliminated "material substance" from empiricism. This was <u>one</u> of the key concepts philosophers had used to explain the world. Hume now turned to another, one that was employed not only by philosophers but also by scientists and by ordinary people of common sense—that of CAUSALITY.

Let's take the sentence "X causes Y," where X and Y are both events. (We'll use Hume's example: X is the event of billiard ball A striking billiard ball B, and Y is the event of ball B moving after being struck.)

1. Is the sentence "X causes Y" analytic?

(That is to say, is the sentence "X does not cause Y" a self-contradiction? Obviously not, because it is perfectly possible to conceive of A striking B and B _not_ moving.)

☑ NO

2. Is the sentence "X causes Y" synthetic?

Now, it seems that the answer will be affirmative because there should be no difficulty in tracing back the idea of "cause" to sense data. But Hume _found_ a difficulty. When he analyzed the concept, he broke it down into three components: (a) priority, (b) contiguity, and (c) necessary connection. "Priority" (the fact that X precedes Y) can be traced to sense data. So can "contiguity" (the fact that X touches Y). But no matter how many times Hume observed ball A strike ball B, he could not find any _necessary connection_ (the fact that if X happens, Y _must_ happen), yet this was exactly what needed to be found if the concept of causality was to be sensible.

Hume Observing Causality

187

So "causality" proved to have the same status as "material substance" and "God." This embarrassment has far-reaching consequences. It means that whenever we say that one thing A causes another B, we are really only reporting our own <u>expectation</u> that A will be followed by B in the future. This is a psychological fact about us and not a fact about the world. But if we try to show the rational grounding of our expectation, we cannot do so. Even if A was followed by B innumerable times in the past, that does not justify our claim to know that it will do so again in the future.

Hume's discovery has come to be known as the PROBLEM OF **INDUCTION**. What makes us so certain that the future will behave like the past? If we answer "because it has always done so in the past," we are begging the question, because the real question is, <u>Must</u> it do so in the future just because it has always done so in the past? Nor can we appeal to "the laws of nature," because then the question is, What guarantees that the "laws of nature" will hold tomorrow? And there is no analytic nor synthetic guarantee of this. Hume concluded from all this that <u>there are no necessary connections between any two events in the universe</u>. This idea leads to what one philosopher has called "dustbowl empiricism"—the view that, on close inspection, reality, like a dust cloud, proves to be composed of discrete, unrelated entities casually (not causally) associated with each other in a tenuous and ephemeral manner.

"Hume's fork" (the analytic/synthetic distinction) has equally disastrous results for the concept of SELF. There is no sense datum to which the concept can be traced. Far from finding the self to be the simple, indubitable, absolutely certain, eternal soul that Descartes had claimed it to be, Hume found, according to his method, that "there is no such idea" as "self." The so-called self proves to be "a bundle or collection of different percep-tions [. . . heat or cold, light or shade, love or hatred, pain or pleasure . . .] which succeed each other with an inconceiv-

**Hume Discovers the Self—
Such as It Is**

able rapidity, and are in a perpetual flux and movement."

David Hume had consistently and vigorously followed the program of empiricism to its logical conclusion. The results were disastrous for the philosophical enterprise. The sphere of rationality was found to be very small indeed, reduced as it was to verbal truths and descriptions of sense data; yet nearly everything that interested people as philosophers or nonphilosophers fell beyond those limits. Hume believed he had shown that human life was incom-patible with rationality and that human endeavors always had to be extrarational, hence irrational. (Rationally, I can never know that the loaf of bread that nourished me yesterday will nourish me today, hence I can never be <u>rationally</u> motivated to eat.) But Hume knew perfectly well that the human being could not be sustained by the meager fruits of philoso-

David Hume—Shepherd

phy. Even while writing his philosophical manuscript he knew that, once he put down his pen, he too would revert to the normal, illogical beliefs of humanity—namely, beliefs in self, world, and causality (if not in God). He even suggested, maybe with tongue in cheek, that perhaps we should abandon philosophy and take to tending sheep instead.

« »

It would be fair to say that the history of philosophy should have ended with Hume if his views had prevailed. To survive Hume's attack, philosophy would need a powerful, subtle, and original mind to come to its defense. It found such a protector in the German IMMANUEL KANT (1724–1804). Kant spent the whole of his life in the old Hanseatic city of Königsberg in the northeastern corner of Prussia (today, Russia) where at least until his fiftieth year, he passed his days complacently in the bourgeois life of a respected professor of the university. This old bachelor, whose personal life was so methodical that his neighbors used to set their clocks by his afternoon walks, had been trained in the rationalistic metaphysics of Christian von Wolff, an undistinguished disciple of Leibniz, and Kant had found no reason to doubt any of its tenets—that is, not until one fine

Herr Professor Immanuel Kant on His Daily Walk

day in his late middle age when a copy of Hume's *Enquiry* crossed his desk. Kant's reading of it "awakened him from his dogmatic slumber," as he later reported. He realized that Hume's powerful argument undermined everything Kant had believed and that no honest progress in philosophy could be made until Hume's skeptical arguments had been refuted.

Kant's response to Hume, and his attempt to synthesize what he took to be the best of Hume's philosophy with the best of what was left of rationalism after Hume's full-scale frontal assault on it, is found in *The Critique of Pure Reason*. There Kant accepted Hume's analytic/synthetic distinction as the key philosophical tool of analysis. Kant agreed with Hume that all analytic propositions are a priori and that all a posteriori propositions are synthetic, but he disagreed with Hume's claim that all synthetic propositions are a posteriori and that all a priori propositions are analytic (hence tautological). That is to say, according to Kant, there is such a thing as a SYNTHETIC A PRIORI TRUTH, a meaningful statement about reality whose truth is known independently of observation.

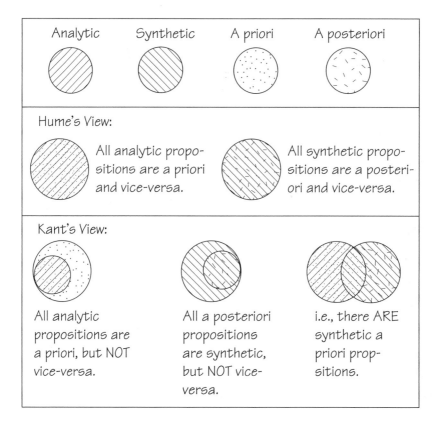

192

Kant believed that only by demonstrating the existence of such truths could Hume be refuted and philosophy, science, and common sense (and perhaps religion) be made respectable again. This would be done by showing that the knowledge that Hume denied was, in fact, grounded in synthetic a priori truth, as were the very arguments that Hume had mustered against such claims of knowledge. Kant began by dividing the mind into three "faculties"—intuition (i.e., perception), understanding, and reason—and then performing what he called a "transcendental" analysis of each faculty.

Kant first dealt with the FACULTY OF INTUITION. Here the primary question which concerned Kant was not "What is perception" nor "Is perception possible?" Rather, it was "How is perception possible?" That is, he began with the commonsense view that we do perceive the world and asked what conditions must hold for that to be possible. For example, he wanted to know how it was possible that we are able to utter true sentences about the height of the Matterhorn if the empiricists were right to say we never perceive SPACE, only sense data. And he wanted to know how it was possible that we are able to utter true sentences about the amount of time it takes to get to Berlin if the empiricists were correct to say we never perceive TIME, only sense data. Kant's solution was to demonstrate that space and time are the synthetic a priori foundations of the faculty of perception. An a posteriori sentence like "The cat is on the mat" presupposes the truth of the sentence "Objects exist in space and time." According to Kant, we sometimes know the first sentence to be true, yet it cannot be true unless the second is also true. The latter is not analytic, and it is not a posteriori (there is no sense datum of space or time—Hume was right about that), so it must be a synthetic a priori truth.

Kant called this method of analysis a "transcendental **deduction**" because it "transcends" direct observation or, better, gets behind and underneath it to discover its necessary conditions. This analysis led Kant to conclude that space and time were not features of external reality. Rather, they were features of the <u>structure</u> <u>of</u> <u>the</u> <u>mind</u>. The human mind analyzes the data it receives in terms of space and time. Space and time are the "irremovable goggles" through which we perceive the world. They are not like

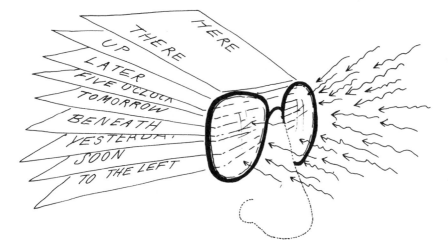

The Irremovable Goggles

pieces on a chess board (things in the world), rather they are like the rules according to which we play chess and in whose absence chess would not exist.

Having discovered the synthetic a priori foundations of the faculty of intuition, Kant then turned to the FACULTY OF UNDERSTANDING. This faculty enables us to understand facts about the world (. . . that Mt. Whitney is higher than Death Valley, . . . that the cat is on the mat). Once again, Kant began not by asking "Can there be knowledge of the world?" Instead, he began with the common-sense assumption that we _do_ have such knowledge and asked how such knowledge was possible. He found that it was grounded in the synthetic a priori foundations of the faculty of the understanding, which he called "the categories of the understanding." These categories included those of UNITY/PLURALITY/TOTALITY, CAUSALITY, and SUBSTANTIALITY. These concepts are not deduced by the mind from reality; on the contrary, the mind brings them to reality. This is why Hume had been unable to find them "out there" when he looked for them. A sentence such as "Every event is caused" (which to Hume was neither empirical nor true by definition) is, according to Kant, a synthetic a priori truth.

Obviously, this theory is reminiscent of the Platonic–Cartesian doctrine of innate ideas, but there is a major difference. Kant did not claim that we are born with a group of _ideas_ but that the mind is structured in such a way that it analyzes its data in terms of a particular set of synthetic _a priori_ _rules_, which are like a permanent program in a computer and which produce ideas when fed information by the senses. If you are a human being, then

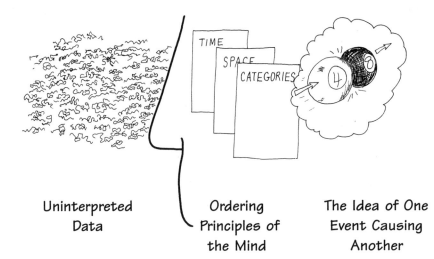

| Uninterpreted Data | Ordering Principles of the Mind | The Idea of One Event Causing Another |

you make sense of the world in terms of such concepts as time/space/substantiality/causality. The mind <u>must</u> order the world in terms of "thingness," though there is nothing "out there" called SUBSTANCE. The mind <u>must</u> understand the world in terms of causal series even though there is nothing out there that is <u>the</u> cause of any event.

Kant's position was meant to represent a compromise between the warring rationalists and empiricists. His famous assertion "thoughts without content are empty, intuitions without concepts are blind" was meant to grant to the rationalists that sense data alone could not provide knowledge and to grant to the empiricists that there could be no knowledge in the absence of sensorial contribution. Kant's solution seemed to many to be successful; however, it had the consequence of putting him in the disconcerting position of admitting that there does exist some kind of ultimate reality (what he called "the noumenal world," or "the thing-in-itself" [<u>das Ding-an-sich</u>]) but that the human mind is incapable of knowing it. Rather, we humans are limited to knowledge of what Kant called "the phenomenal world"—the world as perceived, conceived, imagined, interpreted, analyzed, and theorized about by the human mind. That is, we can only know a world that has passed through the human mind, through the gridwork of space and time and the categories of the understanding. Contrary to Hume's conclusion, for Kant common sense and science are valid but only insofar as their claims are about the phenomenal world. But nothing positive can be said about ultimate reality, other than that it exists. This meant that traditional metaphysics of the type attempted by philosophers from Plato through Leibniz was impossible. Kant deduced this conclusion from his "transcendental" analysis of the faculty of reason.

Kant Peers Beyond the Curtain of the Phenomenal World and Sees Nothing

The FACULTY OF REASON was supposed by Kant to be the faculty that produced the "pure" concepts (i.e., concepts uncontaminated by the senses) such as "God" and "soul." Were there any synthetic a priori foundations for this faculty? (which is another way of asking, can we hope to know any "higher truths" about ultimate reality?). Kant's notorious answer—which was so scandalous to the metaphysicians and theologians—was NO! Traditional metaphysics was impossible because it was always the

The House of Metaphysics Before and After
The Critique of Pure Reason

result of illegitimately applying notions of space, time, and causality to the noumenal world when in fact these concepts can only be applied to the observable world. This is why all proofs of God's existence must fail, along with all attempts to de-scribe ultimate reality in terms of that mysterious category, "substance." We humans must therefore despair of ever knowing of God, justice, immortality, or freedom, since all of these ideas overreach the human capability for knowledge.

If Kant had concluded *The Critique of Pure Reason* at this point, he would have satisfied the Humean critics of metaphysics and theology while pleasing the defenders of common sense and science, but he would not have satisfied those impulses in the human heart toward higher sentiments. To these stirrings, Kant addressed the rest of his *Critique*. There he claimed the following: There is no logical necessity to conceive of the world in terms of God, immortality, justice, and freedom (in the way that there is a logical necessity of conceiving the world in terms of time, space, and causality); nevertheless, without such inspirational concepts, many humans would lose their enthusiasm for life. If one could not believe, for example, that the

human soul is free and that ultimately justice will triumph, then one might well lose the motivation required for the engagement in the day-to-day world. Therefore, according to Kant, one has the right to _believe_ (but not to claim to know) that God, soul, immortality, justice, and freedom exist, not as _metaphysical_ necessities, but as _practical_ (i.e., moral) necessities. We have the right to treat these topics as if they were synthetic a priori truths if doing so will make us better, more successful human beings.

Kant's attempt to distinguish knowledge from belief, yet ground belief in moral necessity, was acceptable to many who were tired of the extravagant claims made by metaphysicians and theologians but who were also looking for a legitimate role for _belief_ in the modern world. Kant's critics, however, accused him of merely "kicking God out the front door in order to let him in through the back door."

After _The Critique of Pure Reason_, Kant wrote a number of other important philosophical works, including _The Critique of Practical Reason_ and _The Foundations of the Metaphysics of Morals_, both of which addressed specifically the problem of ethics. In its emphasis on intention and duty, Kant's theory demonstrated Christianity's influence on him, and in its attempts to ground duty in reason, Kant's theory showed him to be a thinker of the Enlightenment. By positing freedom as if it were grounded in a synthetic a priori truth (for without freedom there can be no moral acts), one can derive an ethical code from its foundations in reason. Being a rule-guided activity, reasoning itself is based on a respect for rules and laws. From such respect, Kant deduced a moral command, which he called the CATEGORICAL IMPERATIVE: "So act that the maxim of your action could be willed as a universal law." All moral acts can be derived from principles that may be universalized without contradiction. Kant thought that, as

creatures of reason, we are duty-bound to obey such principles. Here, we will oversimplify this idea a bit to see what
Kant was talking about.

Let's suppose that you owe a friend five dollars, and
to your annoyance, he pressures you to repay. So you say
to yourself, "If I kill him, I won't have to repay the debt."
But as a true Kantian, you first check to see if you could
universalize the principle governing the proposed action. You
ask yourself, what if everyone accomplished his or her goals
by killing someone? Could there exist a universal law,
"EVERYONE OUGHT TO KILL SOMEONE"? This would be an

impossible law because if everyone complied with it, there
would be no one left to comply with it. Therefore, we are duty-
bound not to kill as a way of solving problems. OK, then
what if you lie to your friend, telling him that you already
repaid the debt? Can the principle behind this proposal be
universalized? Could there be a general law, "EVERYONE
OUGHT ALWAYS TO LIE"? Obviously not because it would be
impossible even to state the law without breaking it.

Therefore, we are duty-bound not to lie. Well, what if you repay the five dollars, then steal them back? Can the principle behind this act be universalized? Imagine a general law saying, "EVERYONE OUGHT ALWAYS TO STEAL."

But this too is an impossible law because the concept of stealing is parasitical upon the concept of <u>property</u>, but if everyone always steals, there can be no property; there can be only temporary possession, that is, stuff passing

Where Theft Is the Law of the Land

from person to person. So we are also duty-bound to refrain from stealing. (If you are a true Kantian, it's beginning to look as though you will have to pay your debt!)

Kant formulated the categorical imperative in a number of ways, not just in terms of the principle of universalizability. One such formulation was this: "So act as to treat humanity, whether in thine own person or in that of any other, in every case as an end withal, never as a means only." By saying we should treat people as ends, and not merely as means, Kant was, of course, admonishing us against using other people as a means to our own ends. He thought that morality entailed the recognition of the dignity of each person as a person. This side of his ethics has widespread practical implications for such issues as sexual relationships, discrimination, informed consent, and death with dignity.

If one dwelt solely on the first formulation of the categorical imperative (the one based on universalizability), Kant's ethics might seem quite bloodless; but this second formulation adds some warmth to his moral doctrine. Nevertheless, there is a bit of coldness at the heart of his view. He was so intent on making morality a question of DUTY that he refused to grant any worth to INCLINATION. According to him, if a person who was motivated by feelings of empathy toward humanity rendered assistance to a helpless, needy person, this act would be of less moral value than would be the same act performed by someone who actually loathed humanity but who was motivated purely by a sense of duty.

Kant's ethical conclusions, like his metaphysical conclusions, were essentially conservative in nature. His theory rationalized all the virtues that his Lutheran upbringing had extolled. (Lutherans had always known that the human's relation to God was one of belief, not of knowledge; and they had always known that they were duty-bound not to murder, lie, or steal.) Nevertheless, it is striking that Kant derived his principles from reason and not from divine commandment. Here he was more of an Enlightenment figure than a Lutheran. And many believe that in saying that certain kinds of metaphysical speculation are a waste of time, Kant revealed something essential about the limits of human reasoning, and in saying that morality requires acts to be viewed from a perspective other than that of self-interest, he revealed something essential about ethics.

VI.
THE 19th CENTURY

If Kant believed that his "critical philosophy" would spell the
end of speculative metaphysics, he was sorely mistaken.
Even during his lifetime, there was emerging a generation of
metaphysicians, some of whom, ironically, were using Kantian
principles to advance their speculations well beyond the limits that Kant lay down in his *Critique*. Kant was especially
embarrassed by the use of his ideas and terminology by
philosophers who were calling themselves Kantians while creating a kind of highly metaphysical idealism of the type
Kant had repudiated. But it must be said that he himself
was somewhat responsible for this turn of events. After all,
he had defined nonhuman reality as a noumenal thing-in-
itself, then announced that it was inaccessible to human
thought, with the consequence that human thought had
access only to itself. As that earlier idealist George
Berkeley would have pointed out, an inaccessible noumenal
world is hardly better than no noumenal world at all. Indeed,
this new generation of German philosophers derived their
idealism from their dissatisfaction with Kant's claim that
there existed a nonmental world that was unknowable.

G. W. F. Hegel

Primary among the ranks of the German idealists were JOHANN GOTTLIEB FICHTE (1762–1814), FRIEDRICH WILHELM JOSEPH VON SCHELLING (1775–1854), and GEORG WILHELM FRIEDRICH HEGEL (1770–1831). Of these, it was Hegel who achieved the greatest prominence, and it will be he who will represent German idealism for us.

Kant had argued that the appearances of ultimate reality are processed by the human mind, which thereby creates a world for us humans to inhabit. Hegel went further and claimed that the mind did not merely <u>structure</u> and <u>regulate</u> reality, but that it <u>generated</u> it and <u>constituted</u> it. That is to say, reality is simply mind or spirit (<u>Geist</u> in German). This left Hegel with a philosophy that he himself called "absolute idealism." It is <u>absolute</u> idealism not only in the sense that absolutely nothing but ideas exist, but also because ultimately Hegel equated "mind" with "divine mind," or "absolute mind." This meant that if MIND = REALITY, then REALITY = GOD. This view, in some ways similar to Spinoza's, made Hegel a pantheist. Furthermore, besides equating <u>Geist</u> with reality and God, Hegel also equated it with HISTORY. Kant had seen the mind as structurally identical from individual to individual, culture to culture, and historical period to historical period. Hegel criticized Kant's view as static and ahistorical. According to Hegel, even though the mind does have a universal, abstract structure, its content changes evolutionarily from period to period. There exists a mode of philosophical introspection that reveals the general structure of Mind and even allows us to reconstruct history in an a priori manner. In our attempt as philosophers to investigate the nature

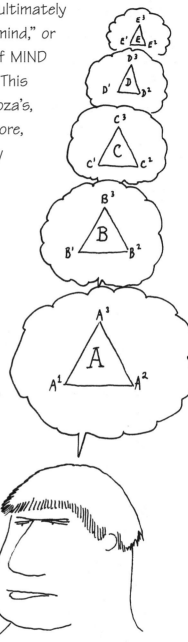

The Evolution of the Mind

of the mind, we can reconstruct the logical (not chronological) beginnings of creation. It goes something like this:

In the beginning, God, pure Mind, and hence pure Being, attempted to think himself. But the thought of pure Being is an impossible thought; therefore, when God attempted to think Being, he thought nothing. That is, he thought the opposite of Being.

But remember, in the unusual system being suggested here, God is God's thought; therefore, in his failure to think pure Being, God has distanced himself from his own essence. This is what Hegel calls God's SELF-ALIENATION. The "truth" of Hegel's insight can be seen in biblical symbolism in the relation between God and Satan. Satan is a fallen angel. He has "fallen away" from divinity. He is, in Hegel's way of thinking, divinity self-alienated. Another biblical indication of Hegel's "truth" can be seen in God's answer to Moses when God spoke to him through the burning bush. When the shrub burst into flame, Moses had asked it, "Who art thou?" and God had answered "I am that which is" (or, in ungrammatical Hebrew, "I am that what am"). Here we see that God cannot say himself without dividing his essence into a subject–object relationship. ("I am ..." [= subject] ☞ "that which is" [= object]. If the subject is the object, then it is not itself as subject.)

Satan Falls Away from God—Divine Self-Alienation—

Hegel's God then is in a kind of identity crisis. But if God experiences an identity crisis, so does the human because the human mind is nothing but a manifestation of the Divine Mind. The history of an individual's mind, like history itself, is the process of self-awareness and self-recovery.

Returning to the dichotomy BEING ←→ NO-THINGNESS—can there be any reconciliation between the two? Well, these two impossible thoughts (neither Pure Being nor Pure Nothingness can truly be

God's Identity Crisis

thought) represent the absolute limitation of all thinking and all reality. That is, all thought and all reality must fall somewhere between these two extremes. Hegel's term for anything occurring between these polar opposites is "Becoming." So we can call "Being" a THESIS (positive, +), "Nothingness" an ANTITHESIS (negative, −), and "Becoming" a SYNTHESIS (combination of positive and negative +/−). This universal structure of all thought and reality Hegel calls the **dialectic.**

SYNTHESIS

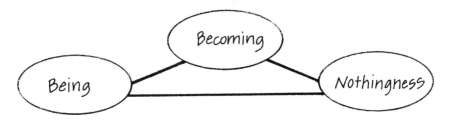

THESIS   ANTITHESIS

Therefore, given anything in the world—a table, for instance—it is in fact a <u>process</u> synthesizing a positivity and a negativity. It <u>is</u> the table by <u>not</u> being the chair or the floor. This is the nature of thought, language, and reality. They are systems of positivities created by negativities, and vice-versa. Every thought, word, and thing exist only as a part of a system of exclusions. Again, a thing is what it is by <u>not</u> being its other, yet that "otherness" is what defines it as a being. This now explains why the thoughts of Pure Being and Pure Nothingness are impossible. Thought and language only function in a system of contrasts, yet Pure Being encompasses all, hence there is nothing to contrast with it, <u>except</u> Nothingness, which is nothing. (Are you following this dizzying "logic"?) Furthermore, it can be deduced from all this that every synthesis must become a new THESIS, and, defined as it is by its opposite, this new thesis must spawn its own ANTITHESIS. So history is an eternal process of the dialectic, with each historical moment being a concatenation of contradictions—the tension between the positive and the negative. These forces are opposed to each other, yet mutually dependent on each other. Eventually, the tension between the thesis and the antithesis destroys the historical moment, but out of its ashes a new historical moment is born, one that <u>brings</u> <u>forward</u> <u>the</u> <u>best</u> <u>of</u> <u>the</u> <u>old</u> <u>moment</u>. Here is Hegel's optimism; there is progress built into history. And if we individuals think we see regression and backsliding at specific times in history, this is because we are blind to "the cunning of Reason," which uses <u>apparent</u> retrograde movements to make hidden progress. Such is the nature of Reason's (i.e., God's) process of self-recovery. Consider, for example, the period of Graeco-Roman democracy. On the one hand, there existed among the Greek and Roman democrats the com-

BECOMING

BEING

HISTORY

NOTHINGNESS

mitment to self-determination, freedom, and human dignity (as seen, e.g., in Pericles' "funeral speech"). On the other hand, during their democratic periods, both Greece and Rome were imperialistic, slave-holding states. These two essential features of the society in question were contradictory but, ironically, were mutually dependent on one another. The slaves existed for the pleasure of the new

democratic class; but, without slavery and the booty from plundering, there never would have been a class of men liberated from toil who could dedicate their time, skills, and intellect to the creation of a democratic state. Yet eventually the <u>conceptual</u> contradiction between freedom and unfreedom, the two pillars of Graeco-Roman democracy, tore the society apart and prepared the way for a new kind of society, medieval feudalism.

Now, feudalism might not seem to you and me like a progression over earlier democratic societies, and, in fact, it might seem like a retrogression. But from Hegel's point of view, medieval society represents an advance in freedom over Greece and Rome because in feudalism there were no slaves. Even the most humble serf had legal rights.

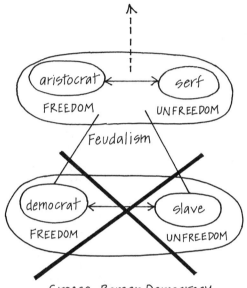

Graeco-Roman Democracy

What happened in history also happens individually. Each of us passes through various stages in our conceptions of our self and our freedom. There is the stage at which we believe we can be free only by escaping the domination of others and by dominating them. Then we come to realize that in dominating them we ourselves are dominated because we become dependent on those we dominate, both materially and in terms of self-identity. (Who am I? I am the lord. But only as long as I am recognized as such by the bondsman. Without his recognition, I would be nobody. Hence, in effect, <u>he</u> is the lord, and I am the bondsman.) Only by acknowledging that neither lord nor bondsman is free can one transcend the unfreedom of relationships of domination and discover higher forms of freedom—which is to say, discover the path of Reason and Divinity.

This is a sample of Hegelian thinking. From it we get an inkling of the psychological, sociological, historical, and theological dimensions of Hegel's thought. What we miss in this sampling is the absolute systematization of his philosophy. An outline of one of his several proposals for such a system follows:

The System

I. The idea-in-itself (= LOGIC)

    A. Being

    B. Nothingness   } [This we've just discussed]

    C. Becoming

II. The idea-outside-itself (= NATURE) [Nature, i.e., the material world qua <u>material</u> is the opposite of spirit but must be <u>potentially</u> spirit. The <u>goal</u> of inanimate matter is spirit.]

III. The idea for itself (= SPIRIT) [The idea recovered from its loss into its opposite.]

    A. Subjective spirit [Mind as self-conscious and introverted.]

    B. Objective spirit [Mind projecting its own laws outward, creating a human world.]

        1. Law [Exterior—comes to the individual from without.]

        2. Morality [Interior—comes from within the individual.]

        3. Ethics [Synthesis of the law exteriorized and interiorized.]

a. Family

b. Society

c. State

C. Absolute spirit

1. Art

2. Religion

3. Philosophy

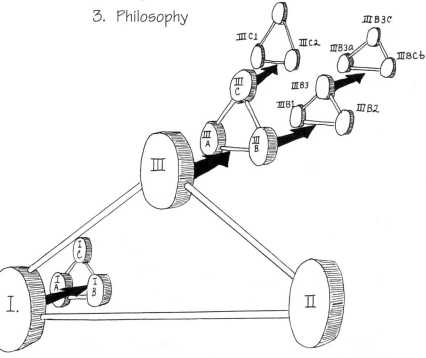

The System

Notice that this whole system is structured in terms of interrelating triads of THESES–ANTITHESES–SYNTHESES (even though Hegel rarely used those terms) and that The STATE is the highest form of "objective spirit." Many of Hegel's critics point this out when they call attention to his eventual worship of the authoritarian, repressive Prussian state. Some even claim his whole system was contrived to be in the political service of the newly restored Prussian monarch, Hegel's paymaster. But it also must be noted that it was not "objective spirit" that is the apogee of Hegel's system, rather it was "absolute spirit," and the highest pinnacle of absolute spirit is not the state but PHILOSOPHY (and, one assumes, particularly Hegel's philosophy).

Hegel triumphant

Arthur Schopenhauer

ARTHUR SCHOPENHAUER (1788–1860) was one of Hegel's sharpest critics. He was a younger contemporary of his who refused to be intimidated by Hegel's immense fame. As a beginning philosophy teacher at the University of Berlin, Schopenhauer had scheduled classes at the same time as

Hegel's, knowing full well that thereby he was guaranteeing for himself few, if any, students. This arrogant young philosopher's opinion of Hegel was one of undisguised contempt, as can be seen in the following unflattering portrait he drew of him.

> Hegel, installed from above by the powers that be as the certified Great Philosopher, was a flat-headed, insipid, nauseating, illiterate charlatan, who reached the pinnacle of audacity in scribbling together and dishing up the craziest mystifying nonsense.

Schopenhauer, in fact, showed deep respect for only two Western philosophers: Plato and Kant. He also admired the philosophical traditions of India. To Schopenhauer, the rest of the philosophers throughout history had been merely "windbags." Schopenhauer began his work demanding a return to Kant, and indeed, the first part of Schopenhauer's main work, *The World as Will and Idea*, was

The History of Philosophy as the History of Windbags

fundamentally a repetition of Kantian ideas. He agreed with Kant that the human mind is incapable of knowing ultimate reality, that the only reality we are capable of grasping intellectually is that which has passed through the grid work of space and time and through the categories of the understanding. Schopenhauer wrote:

> "The world is my idea":—this is a truth which holds good for everything that lives and knows, though man alone can bring it into reflective and abstract consciousness. If he really does this, he has attained to philosophical wisdom. It then becomes clear and certain to him that what he knows is not a sun and an earth, but only an eye that sees a sun, a hand that feels an earth; that the world which surrounds him is there only as idea.

Now, when Kant turned to the noumenal world, he had claimed that we could not know it, though we had the right to hold various beliefs about it based on certain of our practical needs. Recall that for Kant, these beliefs were extremely optimistic ones: faith in God, freedom, immortality, and eternal justice. Furthermore, Kant had pointed out certain human experiences, certain positive intuitions of ours, that he hoped might be extrarational hints about the nature of that unknowable noumenal world. For example, there were those feelings of the sublime that we experience when we look deeply into the sky on a clear summer night, and equally inspiring to Kant were the feelings of moral duty that we experience in certain moments of crisis. As Kant put it, "Two things fill the mind with ever new and increasing admiration and awe . . . the starry heavens above and the moral law within."

Well, Schopenhauer, too, believed that there were certain intuitive experiences that should be heeded because they might well give us an extrarational insight into ultimate reality. But Schopenhauer's examples of such insights were very different indeed from those of Kant.

For example, Schopenhauer wondered why it is that when someone is told of the death of an acquaintance, the first impulse that person experiences is the urge to grin—an urge that, of course, must be suppressed. And Schopenhauer wondered why it is that a respectable businessman or government official, who may have worked tirelessly for years to achieve the success and power that he has finally obtained, is willing to risk all of it for a moment's sexual pleasure with a forbidden partner. These and similar human experiences left Schopenhauer with a much more pessimistic hunch about the nature of ultimate reality than that held by Kant. Schopenhauer's dark suspi-

It's Not Nice to Giggle at Funerals

cions quickly became "truths" in his system. (The curious status of these nonepistemological truths has not escaped the eyes of Schopenhauer's critics.) Said Schopenhauer: "This truth, which must be very serious and impressive if not awful to everyone, is that a man can also say and must say, 'The world is my will.'"

Schopenhauer Peers Beyond the Curtain of the Phenomenal World

Schopenhauer's awful truth amounts to this: Behind appearances, behind the phenomenal veil, there does lie a noumenal reality; but, far from being the benign sphere where Kant hoped to find God, immortality, and justice, Schopenhauer found there a wild seething, inexorable, meaningless force that he called "will." This force creates all and destroys all in its insatiable demand for "More!" (More of _what_ it does not know—it only knows that it wants more.) The best phenomenal images for understanding Schopenhauer's "will" are images of sex and violence. Not only in nature but even in the human sphere, every event is an act of procreation or destruction. Our actions, whether intentional or unintentional, motivated consciously or unconsciously, are, in fact, actions that in one way or another are in the service of procreation and destruction. (It must be obvious to you now where Freud got his idea of the "Id." Even the name "Id" [Latin for "it"] indicates the same noumenal indeterminacy as Schopenhauer's "will." Freud himself said in 1920, "We have unwittingly steered our course into the harbour of Schopenhauer's philosophy.")

According to Schopenhauer, everything in the phenomenal world is merely the manifestation of this perverse will, or, as he called it, an "objectification of the will" (that is to say, the will passed through the categories and the gridwork of space and time).

Even though Schopenhauer's images of the will are ones of dumb brutality, he also conceived of it as immensely cunning. The will is capable of disguising its heartless purposes from any of its own "experiments" that might be capable of taking offense or even taking reprisals against the will. This means that the human mind is constructed in such a way as to be self-deceiving, even concerning its view upon the world. The will is denatured as it passes through the gridwork and the categories. Nevertheless, if we could strip away our natural optimism, itself a product of the "cunning of the will," we could look into nature and see that it cares not a whit for the happiness nor well-being of any of its creatures beyond the bare needs of reproduction.

Schopenhauer illustrated his point with descriptions of the giant turtles of the South Pacific that were known to have been smashed to death by the hundreds against the rocky coast in storms during mating season as they tried to get to shore to lay their eggs in the sand. Schopenhauer also called attention to that strange species of moth that emerges from its cocoon with full reproductive and digestive systems, yet nature forgot to give it one little detail—a mouth! So the moth reproduces, then finds food, but quickly starves to death. Yet nature does not care; the moth has laid its little eggs. And, according to Schopenhauer, what's true of the turtle and the moth is true of the human being. If you are over eighteen years of age, your body is deteriorating. Your body, which is just the scaffolding for the reproductive system, begins to die once it has held its eggs in place and given them a chance to duplicate themselves.

This is terrible news indeed. Why do people not realize that we are all in a state of bondage to the irrational, meaningless will? Precisely because of the cunning of the will. Human culture itself is nothing but one more experi-

The Human Being in the Grip of the Will

Chat Chat Chat
Yak Yak Yak
Bla Bla Bla

AAIIEEEEEE
(SOB) (MOAN)

**What Seems to Be
the Case**

What Is the Case

ment of the will, and human optimism and hope are simply the will's gift to us to guarantee that we continue to deceive ourselves about the true state of affairs. The whole of human culture is nothing more than a grand deception. Art, religion, law, morality, science, and even philosophy are only **sublimations** of the will, sublimations that are still acting in its service. Hegel's glorification of higher culture is simply proof of the absolute triumph of the will.

All of our hopes and aspirations will be dashed. Happiness is an impossible dream. It is absurd that anyone could remain an optimist after even a glance at the newspaper on any given day. A mudslide swallows up whole villages. A mad assassin's bullet strikes down the hope of a people. A single parent, mother of three, is killed by a painful disease. The drums of war never cease beating, and an inglorious death awaits all. Verily, only a fool could remain optimistic in the face of the truth.

Surely philosophy was never so disheartened and disheartening as in the case of Schopenhauer. But, according to him, his pessimism was a <u>rational</u> pessimism, and he sought a rational solution to it. There had, of course, been others who understood the truth and sought rational responses to it. Both Jesus and the Buddha had been pessimists, according to Schopenhauer, but their solutions were chimerical and still in the service of the will (besides, their doctrines were perverted by the cunning of the will manifested in the optimism of their disciples who presented their masters' pessimistic messages as "good news"). Plato too had offered a <u>nearly</u> successful solution, but his eternal Forms were still part of the world of idea, hence of the will.

It might seem that suicide should be the only recommendation that Schopenhauer's philosophy could make. But, in fact, Schopenhauer recommended against suicide on the grounds that self-murder would be a last, desperate act of will, hence still a manifestation of the will (that is to say, no act requires as much concentration of will as does suicide; hence, suicide cannot possibly be the negation of the will).

Plato's Solution

Do not despair! There is a Schopenhauerian solution. Even though all culture is nothing but a sublimation of sex and violence, hence an experiment of the will, there is a point at which the cultural world can achieve such a degree of subtlety that it can break off from its own unconscious origins and set up an independent sphere that is, in fact, counternature and therefore antiwill. This autonomy from the will occurs in a specific corner of the art world—that of music. But not just <u>any</u> music. Certainly, popular music won't do, evoking as it does the imagery and emotions of

Elvis's Solution

the phenomenal world. Nor will most classical music serve. For example, in Beethoven's works, the imagery is still too strong, hence its link to the will is too obvious. (When listening to the <u>Pastoral</u>, we <u>see</u> the cows in the meadow, the bright green grass, and the wildflowers, and the puffy little white clouds in the blue sky.) No, an escape from the will can be achieved only in the contemplation of purely <u>formal</u> music, a music without words and without imagery. There is a kind of baroque

Schopenhauer's Solution

music that fits the bill—a kind of pure mathematical formalism: point, counterpoint, point. It is possible to dedicate one's life to the disinterested contemplation of such music, and Schopenhauer recommended precisely this as his version of Nirvana—an escape from the world into pure form and hence a triumph over the will. It was this toward which Plato and the Buddha were clumsily struggling.

Schopenhauer's philosophy was deeply influential among intellectuals in the German-speaking world. The work of Friedrich Nietzsche, Sigmund Freud, and Thomas Mann is hardly conceivable without Schopenhauer. Yet nobody seems to have taken Schopenhauer's solution very seriously. It was perhaps too obvious, as Nietzsche was to point out, that baroque music is the most sensual of all music and that the desire to immerse oneself in it is after all a <u>desire</u>, hence still the work of the will.

« »

Schopenhauer's method of dealing with Hegel was first to call him names, then to ignore him. But the generation of continental philosophers who followed Schopenhauer had to deal more directly with Hegel, whose influence by the 1830s had become immense. One of the most curious members of this generation was the Dane SØREN KIERKEGAARD (1813–1855). Kierkegaard, who is generally recognized today as "the father of **existentialism**," thought

of himself primarily as a religious author and an anti-philosopher. In truth, he was not opposed to philosophy as such but to <u>Hegel's</u> philosophy. Nevertheless, like the rest of his generation, Kierkegaard fell more under Hegel's spell than he would have liked to admit.

Søren Kierkegaard

Kierkegaard blamed Hegel for much of what he took to be the dehumanization of the intellectual life of a whole generation. This dehumanization was the result of a "correction" that Hegel made to Aristotelian logic. Aristotle had laid down the three basic principles of logic as:

1. The principle of identity (A = A)
2. The principle of noncontradiction [not (A and not–A)]
3. The **principle of the excluded middle** [either (A) or (not–A)]

Hegel believed these principles to be erroneous. His new dialectical logic overturned them. In the dialectic, everything is in some sense its opposite; therefore, it is not the case that A = A because A = not–A. (Greek democracy was in some sense equivalent to Greek slavery, hence it was its own opposite.) If the principle of identity falls, then the principles of noncontradiction and of the excluded middle collapse too. Kierkegaard took offense at the pompousness of Hegel's suggestion. He mocked it with vignettes like the following:

> If you marry, you will regret it; if you do not marry, you will also regret it; . . . whether you marry or do not marry, you will regret both. Laugh at the world's follies, you will regret it; weep over them, you will regret that; laugh at the world's follies or weep over them, you will regret both. . . . Believe a woman, you will regret it, believe her not, you will also regret that; believe a woman or believe her not, you will regret both. . . . Hang yourself, you will regret it, do not hang yourself, and you will also regret that; hang yourself or do not hang yourself, you will regret both. . . . This, gentlemen, is the sum and substance of all philosophy.

This is not really the sum and substance of all philosophy.

I was going to hang myself, but it's just too much trouble.

It is the sum and substance of Hegel's philosophy, a philosophy in which all oppositions are swallowed up, creating absolute apathy and demoralization, and which, by abrogating the principle of the excluded middle, thereby annuls the "either/or" of decision making—and therewith denies freedom, which, for Kierkegaard and his existentialist followers, is the essence of human existence. Therefore, Kierkegaard published the foregoing "ecstatic lecture" in a book which he called *Either/Or*, whose very title was an attack on Hegel.

Not only had Hegel collapsed the distinction between the "either" and the "or," but he had also abolished the difference between epistemology and ontology by asserting "the Real is the Rational and the Rational is the Real," which is another way of saying that existence and thought are identical. Kierkegaard inverted Hegel's assertion, claiming that existence is the one thing that cannot be thought. This is a double-entendre, meaning: (1) Thought and existence are <u>not</u> identical, and (2) it is impossible to think "existence."

Recall that Hegel's god had found himself incapable of thinking pure existence (Pure Being). Kierkegaard pushed this limitation to the fore, claiming not just that pure existence was impossible to think but that <u>any</u> existence was unthinkable. This is because, in Kierkegaard's Platonic theory of meaning, thought is always a form of abstraction. Words are signifiers that denote CONCEPTS, and concepts are general categories. Every word in the sentence "The brown dog obeys its master" denotes for Kierkegaard an abstraction. Language abstracts from experience and suppresses differences in order to allow the possibility of thought and communication; hence, thought (which is language-bound) distances us from real existence, which is never abstract but always <u>concrete</u>.

As opposed to the abstractions of Hegelian philosophy, Kierkegaard's philosophy would return us to the concreteness of existence. But he was not so much interested

Language Alienates One from Lived Experience

231

in the concreteness of existence of things in the world as he was in the concreteness of individual human existence. René Descartes had been right to begin philosophy with the self ("I think, therefore I am"), but he had been wrong, as was Hegel after him, to equate the self with thought. "To think is one thing, to exist is another," said Kierkegaard. I can think and say many things about myself—"I am a teacher, I am a man, I am an American, I am in love, I prefer chocolate to vanilla." Yet, when I am done talking and thinking about myself, there is one thing remaining that cannot be thought—MY EXISTENCE, which is a "surd" (an irrational residue). I

When All the Roles Have Been Stripped Away, What's Left Is My Existence

cannot <u>think</u> it, rather I must <u>live</u> it.

My lived existence, according to Kierkegaard, is equated with passion, decision, and action. None of these categories can be exhausted by thought. But that is not to say that there is no connection between existence and thought. Kierkegaard wrote, "Existence must be interpenetrated with thought." What kind of thought? A kind of philosophical self-consciousness which he called "existential thought."

To explain this notion we must clarify a distinction that Kierkegaard drew in his *Concluding Unscientific Postscript to the Philosophical Fragments* between "objective thought" and "subjective thought." The first category is a kind of thinking for which there exist objective criteria of truth, such as in the case of math, science, and history. If you wonder whether "3 + 2 = 5," "f = ma," or "Caesar crossed the Rubicon in 49 B.C.," there are recognized standards that can be used to determine the truth of these assertions. Objective truths exist, then, but they are "existentially indifferent." That is, they have no essential relationship to my existence. If I found out that one of them was false, I might be surprised, but I would not thereby become a different person. Therefore, Kierkegaard's philosophy is uninterested in "objective truths."

Subjective thought, however, is thought for which there exist no objective criteria of truth. This is so, for example, in the case of VALUES, for instance, ethical and religious claims. If I tell you that it is immoral to cause unnecessary misery to others and if you challenge my assertion, ultimately there are no objective standards for me to appeal to and I cannot prove my claim. (Kantianism won't work, according to Kierkegaard, because it presupposes a valuing of notions of consistency and noncontradictoriness. But what if you refuse to accept that value?) Similarly, if I claim that "God is love" and you challenge me, I cannot appeal to any objective criterion of truth to justify my assertion.

Nevertheless, these "subjective truths" are essential to my existence in the way that "objective truths" are indifferent. This is because we pretty much <u>are</u> what we do, and what we do—the actions we perform—is the result of <u>decisions</u>, which are embodiments of <u>values</u> chosen. Yet those values cannot be grounded in certainty but are always accepted on faith—a faith in the uncertain.

This need for values and decisiveness in the face of the uncertainty of all things provokes, according to Kierkegaard, a kind of dizziness and loss of footing that reveals the true human condition as one of anguish and despair. Hegel was wrong. The real is not the rational. Rather, the lived experience of true human reality

Vertigo in the Face of the Uncertainty of Reality

234

lies underneath rationality as a kind of despairing nothing-ness longing to be a something. (Yet, had Hegel not said this too?)

There are other "subjective truths" besides those of moral and religious valuation. But these truths can only be communicated indirectly, Kierkegaard told us. They can be hinted at, alluded to, overstated, understated, misstated, joked about, poeticized, or ignored. But they cannot be SAID—or at least, if they are said, they can't be directly understood. Such a truth would be the truth of "MY DEATH." Now, I know that all humans die and that, being a human, someday I too will die. I know much about death from the studies I have made in my history and biology classes. But that does not mean that I have grasped <u>my</u> death as a subjective truth. In the *Postscript*, Kierkegaard relates the story of a man who meets a friend on a street corner of Copenhagen and is invited to dinner by him. The invitee enthusiastically promises to attend, but at that very moment the prospective guest is struck and killed by a tile that happens to fall from the roof. Kierkegaard mocks the dead man, saying that one could laugh oneself to death over this case. Here is a person who makes an absolute commitment into the future, yet whose existence is whisked away by a gust of wind. After chuckling for a while over the irony of this story, Kierkegaard then asks himself if he is not being too harsh on the chap. Surely we don't expect the guest to respond to his invitation saying, "I shall attend. Set a place at the table for me, but you must make room for the contingency that a tile falls and strikes me dead, for in that case I shall not attend." Yet the reader of the *Postscript* comes to the realization that is exactly what Kierkegaard wanted. When we reach the understanding that after every utterance we make about the future, we can correctly add the rider: "However, I may be dead in the next moment, in which case I shall not attend," then we will have grasped the subjective truth of <u>our</u> death.

The point of Kierkegaard's story is not to provoke a sense of morbidity. According to him, the discovery of one's death as a subjective truth becomes the pretext for another discovery—that of "one's existence" as a subjective truth. Only against a backdrop of the yawning abyss

The Individual Before the Yawning Abyss of Eternity

of eternity can the immediacy and fragility of existence be understood. Most people are oblivious to the proximity of nothingness, and they spend their lives engaged in petty thoughts and pointless projects. ("Do my socks have holes? What will people think of me if I wear a soiled tie?") But the discovery of our subjective truths concretizes and intensifies our existence. It helps us to order our priorities and clarify our values and to recover the self from its alienation into social roles, material possessions, and linguistic abstractions. It reveals (and at the same time creates) the self that had been invisible to the self.

For Kierkegaard, the self is essentially subjectivity, and subjectivity is constituted by the individual's commitment to his subjective truths. The authentic self, for Kierkegaard, is one that "chooses itself" by a form of self-reflective activity that both clarifies and creates one's values while assuming total responsibility for those values. It was this that Hegel had left out of his system, according to Kierkegaard; or more correctly, it was this that <u>any</u> system would necessarily swallow up. Therefore, Kierkegaard was antisystematic and titled one of his books *Philosophical Fragments*, yet another slap in Hegel's face.

Søren Kierkegaard saw as his task not the development of a new epistemology, nor the creation of a new system of metaphysics, but the creation of a whole new kind of human being, one who could grasp his own freedom and create his own destiny. (In this he was joined by two other wayward nineteenth-century thinkers at whom we have yet to look: Karl Marx and Friedrich Nietzsche.) Kierkegaard calls his version of the new human being "a Knight of Faith." This is a person who, for Kierkegaard, has an almost superhuman kind of strength and greatness. Kierkegaard wrote of the archetypal Knight of Faith,

> Not one shall be forgotten who was great in the world. But each was great in his own way . . . each became great in proportion to his <u>expectation</u>. One became great by expecting the possible, another by expecting the eternal, but he who expected the impossible became greater than all. Everyone shall be remembered but each was great in proportion to the greatness of that with which he <u>strove</u>. For he who strove with the world became great by overcoming the world, and he who strove with himself became great by overcoming himself, but he who strove with God became greater than all.

This knight has grasped the absurdity and contingency of all existence. David Hume had meditated on the disconnectedness of all things. But Hume had <u>only</u> meditated on it while the Knight of Faith feels it in his bones. yet he finds the strength within himself to unify his world, to hold it together

That Other "Knight of Faith"

with an act of will, which Kierkegaard called "faith." He is an individual who has looked profoundly into the world of men and seen that at the deepest level we are alone—in "absolute isolation"—an aloneness that constitutes a kind of madness, "divine madness," for Kierkegaard's hero is alone with his god. In fact, Kierkegaard's Knight of Faith, his "new human," is not new at all. Rather, he is based on Kierkegaard's tortured interpretation of the biblical patriarch Abraham, who heard a voice in the night telling him to sacrifice his son. Abraham took full responsibility for the meaning of the message—it was <u>his</u> meaning, his subjective truth—and for his actions, thereby becoming a Kierkegaardian hero. Kierkegaard wrote of him, "Abraham was greater than all, great by reason of his power whose strength is impotence, great by reason of his wisdom whose secret is foolishness, great by reason of his hope whose form is madness." Hegel had transformed human existence into pure thought. Kierkegaard counteracted Hegel's rationalization by introducing into philosophy a new category, "the category of the absurd," and putting it in the heart of his ideal human being.

Of course, Søren Kierkegaard was not the only philosopher of his generation to be deeply influenced by Hegel. When KARL MARX (1818–1883) arrived as a young philosophy student at the University of Berlin in the mid-1830s, Hegel had been dead of cholera for five years, but his spirit still reigned supreme. To do philosophy in the Germany of the 1830s was to do Hegelian philosophy. Nevertheless, the Hegelians were by no means in agreement as to what

Hegel's Spirit Reigns Supreme

"doing philosophy" truly consisted of. In fact, they had broken into two warring camps, the "Hegelian Left" and the "Hegelian Right." The Right gave the more orthodox reading of Hegel and was composed mostly of older, more conservative members of their generation. They were primarily interested in what Hegel had to say about religion and morality. The Left was composed of younger, more radical philosophers. They sometimes called themselves "the Young Hegelians." They were mostly interested in developing what they took to be still inchoate Hegelian notions about social and political issues. They believed that Hegel's ideas as he himself understood them were false but that there was a hidden truth in them that needed revealing. Their attitude toward Hegel's writing was very much like Freud's attitude toward dreams. There is a "manifest content" (the dream images) and a "latent content" (the true meaning of the dream, which can be discovered only by interpreting the manifest content). As with Freud, sometimes the analysis

The Manifest Content

The Latent Content

of the imagery demonstrates that its meaning is the opposite of what it appears to be.

Needless to say, Marx fell under the influence of the Hegelian Left, not the Right. The foremost practitioner of the art of Hegelian Leftism was LUDWIG FEUERBACH (1804–1872), whose *Essence of Christianity* became holy scripture to a whole generation of progressive German youth.

Feuerbach's book, which was meant to be a kind of anthropological analysis of religion, contained an inversion of a key Hegelian idea. Hegel had asserted, "Man is God self-alienated." Feuerbach reversed this proposition, saying, "God is man self-alienated." That is, the idea of God is the perversion of the idea of man. Feuerbach believed that there were certain (Platonic) universal values to which all humans aspired. Every culture throughout history has

longed for truth, beauty, justice, strength, and purity. It is part of the human essence to have these longings. But as historical peoples were frustrated in their attempts to achieve these ideals, the ideals themselves became alienated from the human and were projected onto an Ideal Being, a God who demanded that all be sacrificed to his glory. For

Feuerbach, as long as we humans continued to alienate our ideals into some nonhuman extraneous being, we would never be able to achieve the fullness of our own being. Hegel had caught only a glimpse of the truth. Man is God, but he can only become the god that he is by an act of self-recovery that can be brought about exclusively by annuling our traditional concept of religion. For example, consider the Feuerbachian concept of "the Holy Family":

According to Feuerbach, only by abolishing the image of the heavenly family can we bring peace, happiness, and love into the earthly family, because as long as we hold the image of the former before us, we will consider the earth

This is the HEAVENLY FAMILY. It is the idealization of the earthly family. Here peace, happiness, and love reign.

This is the EARTHLY FAMILY. The frustrated father comes home drunk from the tavern where he has spent much of the pittance that is his weekly wage. He expends his rage terrorizing his wife and children.

merely a place of trial and punishment. The worker will attend church on Sunday, confess his sins, become resigned to misery as the human lot, and on the next pay-day return to the tavern to drink away his meager salary.

Marx fell directly under Feuerbach's influence. As a young philosophy student, Marx wrote, "One cannot do philosophy without passing through the fiery brook." (In German, Feuerbach means "fiery brook.") But Marx soon became disenchanted with Feuerbach, and his own philosophy began with a critique of his old mentor. Feuerbach had prided himself on having escaped from Hegel's idealism, proclaiming himself a materialist. But Marx criticized Feuerbach as a crypto-idealist, that is, an idealist who believes himself to be a materialist. Marx pointed out the idealistic implications of Feuerbach's account of the heavenly family. According to it, we could bring about changes in the MATERIAL configurations of the earthly family by changing the IDEA of the heavenly family. Marx, to the contrary, argued that all change must begin at the level of material configurations. In his *Theses Against Feuerbach*, he wrote, "Once the earthly family is discovered to be the secret of the holy family, the former must then itself be theoretically criticized and radically changed in practice." Consistent with this attitude, Marx ended his tract against Feuerbach with the following famous line: "The philosophers have only interpreted the world in various ways: the point however is to change it." Marx believed that once the family was revolutionized (i.e., once its hierarchy of power was restructured, along with the hierarchy of power in the society of which the family was the mirror image), then the idea of the holy family would simply disappear. Religion would not need to be abolished; it would simply dissolve. This is because, contrary to Feuerbach, religion is not the <u>cause</u> of alienation; it is, rather, a <u>symptom</u> of alienation and sometimes even a remonstration against it. Marx's statement that religion is the opiate of the masses is often taken out of context and misunderstood. What he actually said in *The German Ideology* is this: "<u>Religious</u> distress is at the same time the <u>expression</u> of real distress and the <u>protest</u> against real distress. Religion is the sigh of the oppressed

The Disappearance of the Heavenly Family

creature, the heart of a heartless world, just as it is the spirit of an unspiritual situation. It is the <u>opium</u> of the people." Here the word <u>opium</u> refers to the drug's medicinal powers.

Like Feuerbach and Hegel before him, Marx was interested in analyzing **alienation** (the process of the subject being split from its natural object). Although Marx discussed alienation in a number of its manifestations (alienation from nature, social alienation, and self-alienation), he was most philosophically original perhaps in his account of "the alienation of labor." Marx believed that it was of the nature of human beings to be producers. We create of necessity, Marx thought. He preferred the designation _homo_ _faber_ (man the maker) to _homo_ _sapiens_ (man the knower) because our _knowing_ is dependent on our _doing_. According to Marx, to a great extent we are what we make. We create our products and our products re-create us. Our minds begin to take on the features of the objects we create. If we create in piecemeal, fragmented ways, we become piecemeal and fragmented ourselves. If we

You Are What You Make

create useless objects, we ourselves become useless human beings. Unfortunately, the processes of production are influenced by historical forces which are not always in our control. When these forces, usually socio-politico-economic ones, drive a wedge between individual humans and their products, the result is "alienated labor." This happens if the work one performs is not the expression of a natural creative need but is motivated by the necessity of fulfilling other needs, such as economic or avaricious ones. Further alienation occurs if the product one creates is for the profit of another and if the product enters into an economic system meant to fulfill desires of greed rather than true human needs. And above all, alienated labor comes about if the worker's product returns to the worker as a

The Worker Confronts Himself as an Alien

disabling alien force. (Extreme case: The worker produces cigarettes, which give him lung cancer.) It will come as no surprise to you to hear that, according to Marx, of all the historical socioeconomic systems, with the exception of slavery, capitalism is the one that promotes the most intense forms of alienated labor.

Alienated labor, in turn, produces self-alienation—the worker confronts himself as a stranger and as a stranger to the human race. (This is Marx's version of Hegel's divine identity crisis.) The goal of the young karl Marx's communism was to create a society in which all alienation would be overcome and where humans would recover their lost essence as _homo_ _faber_.

In converting Hegel's idealism into a form of materialism (thereby "standing Hegel on his head"), Marx created a philosophy unique in his-

Marx Stands Hegel on His Head

tory. We have run across materialists before, of course; Democritus and Hobbes were such. But each of them, in claiming that ultimately everything resolves into matter, chose to define his key category in terms of physics. Their "material reality" was simply mass in motion. But Marx chose his key category not from physics but from economics. He did not try to explain the whole of reality but only human reality. Marx used an analytic model involving a <u>foundation</u> and a <u>superstructure</u>. According to him, the foundations of the social world are material ones: natural

resources, means of production, and means of distribution, as well as the human work relations involved at this level. Built on this foundation, there is a level composed of certain other social relations, such as legal and political arrangements, and above this there is yet another level comprising "higher culture": such social features as art, religion, morality, poetry, and philosophy. In *A Contribution to the Critique of Political Economy*, Marx wrote:

> In the social production of their life, men enter into definite relations that are indispensable and independent of their will, relations of production which correspond to a definite stage of development of their material productive forces. The sum total of these relations of production constitutes the economic structure of society, the real foundation, on

which rises a legal and political superstructure and to which correspond definite forms of social consciousness. The mode of production of material life conditions the social, political, and intellectual life process in general. It is not the consciousness of men that determines their social being, but, on the contrary, their social being that determines their consciousness.

In this and similar passages, Marx made the relationship between the foundation and the superstructure seem simple. Higher culture, or what he called the "ideological" sphere, was merely a "reflex" or a "sublimate" of the socioeconomic foundation. Later he modified this, admitting

Portrait of Louis XIV
(after Hyacinthe
Rigaud)

Laws Establishing
Aristocratic Privilege
(e.g., antipoaching laws)

Property Ownership by
the Nobility

Art as Ideology

that the ideational superstructure and the material foundation mutually influenced each other, though ultimately it was the foundation that dominated. The ideational features of society never ceased to be **ideology**, that is, a system of unconscious propaganda for the foundational economic structure. Therefore, to find out the true status of the symbols in a society, one simply asks, "Who owns the foundation?" Find out who controls the natural resources, the means of production, and the means of distribution (the raw materials, the factories, the trucking lines, and distribution outlets), and you will discover the secret behind the laws, the politics, the science, the art, the morality, and the religion of any society. As the old saw has it, "He who pays the piper calls the tune." Marx's version is, "The ruling ideas of each age have ever been the ideas of its ruling class."

Add to Marx's materialistic model of "foundation and superstructure" his dialectical interpretation of the foundation. The possession of a society's material wealth by a specific group of people automatically creates a class system—basically, the owning class (the "haves") and the class controlled by the owning class (the "have nots"). Since the interests of these two classes are always in opposition, these classes must be in perpetual conflict. In the first line of *The Communist Manifesto*, Marx announced, "The history of all hitherto existing society is the history of class struggle." This conflict, which began in prehistoric times with the creation of tools, had, in Marx's time, reached what he took to be its most clearly delineated stage, and indeed, according to him, it had reached its final stage, a struggle between the owning class of

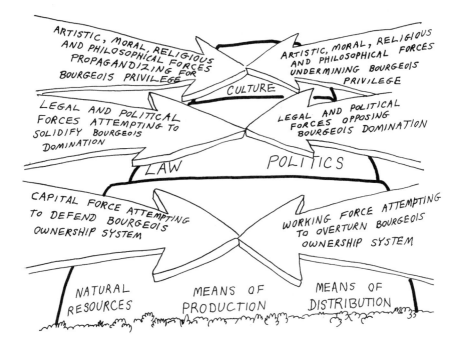

ARTISTIC, MORAL, RELIGIOUS AND PHILOSOPHICAL FORCES PROPAGANDIZING FOR BOURGEOIS PRIVILEGE

ARTISTIC, MORAL, RELIGIOUS AND PHILOSOPHICAL FORCES UNDERMINING BOURGEOIS PRIVILEGE

CULTURE

LEGAL AND POLITICAL FORCES ATTEMPTING TO SOLIDIFY BOURGEOIS DOMINATION

LEGAL AND POLITICAL FORCES OPPOSING BOURGEOIS DOMINATION

LAW   POLITICS

CAPITAL FORCE ATTEMPTING TO DEFEND BOURGEOIS OWNERSHIP SYSTEM

WORKING FORCE ATTEMPTING TO OVERTURN BOURGEOIS OWNERSHIP SYSTEM

NATURAL RESOURCES   MEANS OF PRODUCTION   MEANS OF DISTRIBUTION

capitalism—the bourgeoisie—and the working class that capitalism exploited—the proletariat. Marx spent the bulk of his mature years describing the structure of capitalism in all of its internal contradictions (memories of the Hegelian dialectic!), for example, capitalism's emphasis on competition leading to its own opposite, monopoly—and the consequent expulsion of some former members of the economic elite into the ranks of the paupers; capitalism's constant need for new sources of raw materials, cheap labor, and dumping grounds for its products—leading to imperialistic wars among capitalist states; capitalism's need to solve the problem of unemployment, achieved by pumping more money into the system, thereby creating inflation, and its need to solve the problem of inflation, achieved by increasing unemployment. Marx thought that these internal contradictions of capitalism, along with the massive unrest that would be caused by the ever-growing misery of its dispossessed, would necessarily bring on a simultaneous internal collapse of capitalism and a revolt of the working class that would produce Marx's notorious "dictatorship of the proletariat," whose function it would be to ensure that the victorious proletariat did not reconstitute the institutions of

As per Karl Marx's Prediction, Capitalism Collapses in the Middle Due to Its Own Excesses

classism. (After all, these conquering street fighters themselves grew up in conditions of alienation and hence in **"false consciousness."**) According to Marx, once this dictatorship has performed its essential service, it will simply step down from power—"wither," as Marx had it. Marx's critics are quick to point out that he does not deal with the question of the abuse of power in his socialistic utopia. Perhaps this is due to the philosophical optimism he inherited from Hegel. Unfortunately, as the Stalinist period in the Soviet Union proved, Lord Acton's pessimism was more realistic than Marx's optimism. (It was Acton who said, "Power corrupts, and absolute power corrupts absolutely.") This relinquishing of control by the dictatorship will usher in a classless society, which will end the dialectic of conflict and therefore end history as we know it. (History was defined, after all, as "the history of class conflict.") Humans will live under optimum conditions for

the first time since aboriginal times. Private ownership will be abolished, as well as "the division of labor" (i.e., the type of specialization where one is defined throughout life by the practice of <u>one</u> speciality). We will all be artists and philosophers, and we will "hunt in the morning, fish in the afternoon, rear cattle in the evening, criticize [poetry] after dinner, just as [we] have in mind, without ever becoming hunter, fisherman, shepherd or critic." Elsewhere Marx includes in his picture of the ideal world: socializing in the pub, going to dances, going to the theater, buying books, loving, theorizing painting, singing, and even fencing.

The New Golden Age?

(Fencing?) Sometimes Marx's "true communist society" seems more like a bourgeois pastoral than a working-class paradise; and sometimes, as in the case of Kierkegaard, his "new human being" seems to be a very "old human being," though not one from the historical past, but from the mythical Golden Age.

Friedrich Nietzsche

FRIEDRICH NIETZSCHE (1844–1900) was the third post-Kantian who responded to the crisis of his time not by demanding a new "critique of reason" but by calling for a new kind of human existence. (The other two, as we have seen, were Kierkegaard and Marx.) Nietzsche was a solitary thinker who liked Alpine trails more than the halls of academia (which he abandoned in his mid thirties). He spent most of his life using his authorship in an attempt to triumph over the powerful influences on his childhood: Lutheranism, German nationalism, and the domination of his forceful mother, granny, aunts, and sister. (His attempts were more successful in some of these endeavors than in others.) The material result of his efforts was an unprecedented stream of the most eccentric books ever to have been introduced into the history of philosophy, including such titles as *The Birth of Tragedy*, *Beyond Good and Evil*, *The Genealogy of Morals*, *Thus Spoke Zarathustra*, and his outrageous intellectual autobiography, pretentiously titled *Ecce Homo* ("behold the man"—the phrase with which Pilate introduced Jesus to the masses), with such chapter headings as "Why I Am So Wise," "Why I am So Clever," and "Why I Write Such Good Books." Nietzsche's short, prolific authorship ended in 1888 with the onset of syphilis-induced insanity.

Nietzsche's epistemological theory constituted a radical return to the sophistic period. It is usually called "perspectivism." It derived from Nietzsche's early training as a philologist. Philologists, those students of ancient languages, knew that what was called *The Bible*, *The Vedas*, *The Upanishads*, or *The Iliad* were not direct translations of single existing documents; rather, they were compilations of fragments of conflicting evidence derived from a dizzying number of sources. The dream of the philologists was to find <u>the</u> original texts of each of the great scriptures in history. Nietzsche's conclusion as a philologist was that <u>there</u> <u>is</u> <u>no</u> <u>original</u> <u>text</u>. Each of

There is no original text.

these books is simply the result of a <u>decision</u> to let a particular interpretation represent an end product, even though in fact that "end product" is merely an emblem of a relationship that exists among a number of fragmentary documents, reports, historical studies, and items of gossip.

Nietzsche translated his philological insight into an ontological and epistemological doctrine. Just as in **philology** there is no original text, so in reality and knowledge there is no "pure being" nor "original datum." There are no gods, no Platonic Forms, no substances, no "things-in-themselves," nor even any "things." There exist only flux and chaos upon which we must impose our will. Therefore, said Nietzsche, there can be no such thing as <u>knowing</u> in the Platonic sense. All "knowing" is inventing, and all inventing is lying. But then, there are lies, and there are <u>lies</u>. Inauthentic lying is <u>self</u>-deception. According to Nietzsche, self-deceivers are those who "lie traditionally," that is, who lie in terms of established traditions.

Nietzsche's recommendation in the face of what appears to be a condemnation to a life of lying is to "lie creatively," which is to say to invent, or "know," creatively. To do this is to express what Nietzsche, borrowing and subverting a

Forcing Reality to Bend to One's Will

Schopenhauerian idea, calls "will to power." To express will to power is to force "reality" to submit to one's own creative might. Nietzsche also calls will to power "the urge to freedom." All of our biological instincts expend themselves as manifestations of this desire for freedom, even though in most cases these instincts have been constrained by the forces of normalization (themselves other manifestations of will to power, or, manifestations of the will to power of <u>others</u>).

Not only our biology but also our thought and language are manifestations of will to power. But at the same time, language and thought are the main vehicles of self-deception. According to Nietzsche's radical account of language (reminiscent of Kierkegaard's), language functions

precisely by lying, that is, by denying real dissimilarities and inventing fictitious similarities. For example, the only way we can classify as "leaves" all the forms of foliage that sprout from trees and shrubs is by ignoring and, indeed, <u>suppressing</u> the fact that no two of these entities are alike and by asserting an identity among them that does not, in fact, exist. So language can be and usually is a medium of **reification** and petrification of being. It produces errors that "tyrannize over us as a condition of life." But the fact that language <u>must</u> lie is also the source of the creative possibilities inherent in language. Nietzsche rejected the traditional view of language, namely, that its poetic function is peripheral to its literal function. He felt that the so-called literal function was merely a subclass of its poetic nature. Language, according to Nietzsche, is "a mobile army of metaphors, metonyms and anthropomorphisms." [Reminder: A metaphor is a form of speech in which one image replaces another, importing the new meaning into the old context. ("Achilles is a lion in battle.") A metonym is a form of speech in which meaning is displaced from one image onto an adjacent image that now bears the weight of both images. ("He likes the bottle too much.") **Anthropomorphisms**—the projection of human traits onto the nonhuman world ("The rose is striving to reach the light")—are themselves usually unconscious metaphors or metonyms.] There can be whole chains of metaphors and metonyms that create a poetic rendition

Language: A Mobile Army of Metaphors, Metonyms, and Anthropomorphisms

of reality. Nietzsche recognized these as felicitous expressions of will to power.

In fact, as Nietzsche understood full well, his own term "will to power" was the product of such a metaphorical/metonymical chain of reasoning, as were his other key terms, such as "the overman," "eternal recurrence," and "the death of god." It follows, then, that a claim of Nietzsche's—such as this: "All being is Will to Power"—constitutes not a philosophical insight into the ultimate nature of being but simply another poetic interpretation of being. (When confronted with this charge, Nietzsche responded, "Well, all the better!")

If it is true that there are only interpretations, are all interpretations equally valid? It is clear that, despite his relativism, Nietzsche did not think so. Only those "lies" that affirm life are truly noble lies for him. All other lies are nihilistic and on the side of death. This is why will to power must be full of laughter, dancing, and affirmation and why we must condemn Platonism ("that fear of time") and Christianity ("Platonism for the masses"), which in longing for another world deny reality as it is (i.e., they refuse to recognize reality as chaos and flux that must be molded in the image of each will), and thereby long not for being but for nothingness and death. (One smells Hegel in all this, somehow.) Nietzsche embodied his doctrine in a goal that he called "the overman" (der Übermensch). The overman represents the triumph of the will to power. Besides teaching laughter and dance, the overman teaches "the death of God" and "eternal recurrence." Of course, there can be no single correct answer to the question, "what did Nietzsche mean by 'the death of God'?"

Der Übermensch?

(anymore than there can be to the question concerning
what Prufrock meant when he said, "I should have been a
pair of ragged claws scuttling across the floors of silent
seas"), but surely Nietzsche at least meant to announce
the end of traditional forms of authority: historical, political, religious, moral, and textual. (For an interesting reading
of Nietzsche's phrase, "*God is dead*," try replacing the

The Death of Santa Claus

term "God" with the term "Santa Claus." Why is the claim "Santa Claus does not exist" less tragic than the claim "Santa Claus is dead"?)

What is true of "the death of God" is true of "eternal recurrence." There has been a great river of literature trying to interpret this enigmatic doctrine. But whatever else it means, it was certainly meant to assert Nietzsche's allegiance to reality as it is. Nietzsche advocated what he took to be the opposite of the Schopenhauerian ideal of pessimism, namely,

> the ideal of the most high-spirited, alive and world-affirm-ing human being who has not only come to terms and learned to get along with whatever was and is, but who wants to have <u>what</u> <u>was</u> <u>and</u> <u>is</u> repeated into all eternity. . . . Let us think this thought in its most terrible form: existence as it is, without meaning or aim, yet recurring

264

inevitably without any finale of nothingness: the <u>eternal recurrence.</u>

It is easy enough to criticize Nietzsche for his inconsistency and faulty logic. (How can we will life as it really is if there is no such thing as life nor will—only interpretations of interpretations? If everything is a lie, then isn't the claim

The Thought in Its Most Terrible Form:
The Eternal Recurrence

that everything is a lie also a lie?) But this misses Nietzsche's point. He meant to teach neither consistency nor logic but a radically new kind of subversive subjectivity that would undermine all previous forms of thought and being. However, there is a price to pay for such subversiveness. One will have disciples that one might not have hoped for. And indeed, many diverse groups have claimed the Nietzschean heritage, including Nazis, psychoanalysts, existentialists, and currently, a group called "deconstructionists," whom some see as the new liberators and others as the new nihilists.

« »

Let us leave the extravagant frenzy of Nietzsche's (ultimately) deranged mind and turn to the orderly and complacent minds of his contemporaries in the British Isles (whom Nietzsche dismissed as "blockheads"). Despite Hume's facetious suggestion that philosophy be abandoned altogether, a philosophical empiricism was alive and thriving in mid-nineteenth-century Britain. It derived from a side of Hume's thought,

Nietzsche's View of a Meeting of the Utilitarian Society

which was not explored in this book and which is difficult to square with his radical skepticism. Despite his denial of the possibility of true knowledge concerning causality, self, and the external world, Hume held that what is commonly taken as "knowledge" in these areas is really a set of reasonable beliefs that are well founded because they are based on experience. The tradition deriving from this more practical side of Hume was inherited by a group of philosophers known as the UTILITARIANS, headed by JEREMY BENTHAM (1748–1832) and his wayward follower JOHN STUART MILL (1808–1873), who were interested in applying the principles of empiricism to moral and social issues. The eccentric Bentham (whose fully dressed, mummified body still presides over the trustees' meetings at University College in London because his fortune was left to them

**John Stuart Mill with the Mummified
Head of Jeremy Bentham**

with the provision that he be able to attend all of their meetings) concluded that all theory, including moral and political theory, must be grounded in empirical fact. He claimed that in the case of the human sciences this fact would have to be the primacy of the pleasure principle. That is to say, all analyses of human behavior and all recommendations for change in behavior would have to begin with the fact that humans are motivated by the desire for pleasure and by the aversion to pain. In this, of course, he was not unlike Hobbes, though Bentham's conclusions were much more liberal.

The doctrine that only pleasure can (or should) have value is known as HEDONISM, and we have seen this philosophy before, not just with Hobbes but also with Epicurus and Callicles. Bentham's innovation was the claim that hedonism doesn't have to be egoistic; it can be social. That is, one can (and should) be motivated to act in the name of the pleasure of others as well as for one's own pleasure. His SOCIAL HEDONISM is reflected in his most famous maxim, "The greatest amount of happiness for the greatest number" (where "happiness" is defined in terms of pleasure). This principle, in association with the "one person, one vote" principle (i.e., each person gets to define his or her version of happiness), gave Bentham's utilitarianism a distinctly democratic cast. Furthermore, it meant that the moral worth of an act depended exclusively on the amount of happiness or unhappiness that the act promoted. This view is sometimes called "consequentialism" (because it is the consequence of the act that determines the act's value), and it is the opposite extreme from Kant's moral perspective, according to which the moral worth of an action depended on the <u>intention</u> of the agent, on whether the act was motivated by a desire to do one's duty, and on whether the act was consistent with the laws of rationality.

Kant and Bentham between them have provided us with the two key moral models used in Western ethics. Unfortunately, the conclusions drawn from these two models sometimes contradict each other, and, when applied to specific cases, sometimes the utilitarian view seems much more reasonable than the Kantian one; yet in other cases, the Kantian view seems better than the utilitarian one. For instance, the Kantian ethic tells us we are duty-bound never to lie. But what if an armed man, frothing at the mouth, asks us where Bill Jones is? Do we have a duty to tell the truth, knowing full well that doing so may lead to Jones's death? Here Bentham's principle seems better: The act of lying is not immoral if by lying we can prevent grievous harm. But consider another famous example: What if you pay a visit to a friend in the hospital, and a utilitarian physician decides to sacrifice you and distribute your vital organs to five patients who will die if they do not receive immediate organ implants? The doctor is acting on the "greatest amount of happiness for the greatest number of people" principle and maybe even on the "one person, one vote" principle. But in this case, most of us probably feel that Kant would be right to call this sacrifice immoral.

As we saw, Bentham believed that happiness could be defined in terms of pleasure, and he held that the study of pleasure could be refined to a science. Pleasures could be experienced in terms of seven categories. These categories could be articulated in terms of a set of seven questions:

1. INTENSITY (How intense is the pleasure?)

2. DURATION (How long does the pleasure last?)

3. CERTAINTY (How sure is the pleasure?)

4. PROXIMITY (How soon will the pleasure be experienced?)

5. FECUNDITY (How many more pleasures will follow in the train of this pleasure?)

6. PURITY (How free from pain is the pleasure?)

7. EXTENT (How many people will experience the pleasure? [It is this category that makes Bentham's hedonism a <u>social</u> one.])

When considering any act whatsoever, one should analyze it in terms of the pleasure it will produce in these seven categories, which Bentham called "The calculus of felicity."

On a scale of one to ten, this is about a "ten" in all categories.

He thought that after some practice one could learn to apply this calculus rather intuitively, but until that point, one should actually work out the figures as often as possible. (Indeed, the story gos that he himself did this in choosing between remaining a bachelor or marrying. [He married!]) Try out the calculus on a decision such as that between studying for a chemistry midterm exam and going to the beach with some friends. Obviously, the beach party will be strong in some categories (1, 3, 4, 6), and weaker in others (2, 5). Studying will be weak in most categories but strong in a few (2 and 5, and 7 also, if other persons have an interest in your succeeding in college). Are the assets of studying strong enough to overcome its deficits, in the face of the fun enticing you to the beach? (Of course, the guilt you would experience at the beach has to be taken into consideration too.) According to the "one person, one vote" principle, each person must decide for himself or herself.

Beach Guilt

JOHN STUART MILL, who was raised in strict adherence to Benthamite tenets, developed certain qualms about those views after suffering a nervous breakdown at twenty-one years of age. Among other concerns, he was worried about the beach/chemistry–type decision, or perhaps more about the six-pack of beer/Shakespearean sonnet–type decision. If the average person were given the choice between reading a Renaissance poem or guzzling beer while watching the Forty-Niners on the tube . . . well, you can't force people to read poetry or watch football if they don't think it's fun. But in a democracy, under the "one person, one vote" principle, what if you gave people a choice of making public expenditures for the teaching of Shakespeare in universities <u>or</u> receiving a tax rebate? Mill feared the worst and thought it bode ill for the advancement of civilization. If we let ourselves be guided by the calculus of felicity, perhaps the pig would prove to be right; wallowing in the mud might rank higher than studying philosophy.

Mill solved the problem by saying that only those who were competent judges of <u>both</u> of two competing experiences could "vote" for one or the other of them. (You get a vote only if you know beer <u>and</u> Shakespeare or have wallowed <u>and</u> read Plato.) Mill's conclusion was that "some kinds of pleasure are more desirable and more valuable than others." One assumes that he had in mind the reading of Shakespeare and Plato.

Mill claimed that in abandoning the calculus of felicity, he was simply defining pleasure in qualitative and not merely quantitative terms. His critics charge, however, that in asserting that some pleasures are better than others, Mill had abandoned the "principle of utility" (i.e., the pleasure principle) altogether. They have also charged him with elitism and with undermining the democratic foundation that Bentham had given utilitarianism. For what it's worth, Mill's doctrine did leave us some questions to ponder: In a democracy, must the "one person, one vote" principle apply at all levels of decision making? And if so, are democracy and higher culture compatible?

In his most famous book, *On Liberty*, Mill outlined his doctrine of <u>laisser-faire</u> (hands off!). There were certain spheres where the government had no business interfering in the lives of its citizens. Mill's "principle of liberty" states, ". . . the only purpose for which power can be rightfully exercised over any member of a civilized community, against his will, is to prevent harm to others." In other words, Mill was against "state paternalism," the condition in which the state orders a citizen what to do for his or her own good. For Mill, there could be no such thing as a "victimless crime." If a man decides to ride his Harley without a helmet, get bombed on "Ripple" or drugs in the privacy of his own house, visit a prostitute, or even <u>become</u> a prostitute, that's his own business and not the state's.

A Drunken Male Prostitute Without a Helmet Riding His Motorcycle in the Privacy of His Own Home

For moral reasons, we should perhaps try to persuade him of the error of his ways, but we have no business passing laws to protect him from himself as long as he is doing no harm to others. (Contemporary commentators point out that it was probably easier to draw this distinction in Mill's day than in our own. In today's world, there are very few acts that are purely private. If you go to a hospital because of a motorcycle injury, my tax dollars may well have to nurse you back to health.)

Mill also believed in the "hands-off" doctrine in the marketplace. He said, "<u>Laisser-faire</u> . . . should be the general practice: every departure from it, unless required by some great good, is a certain evil." He thought that under most conditions, the government should not interfere in the exchange of commodities, that the law of supply and demand should determine the nature and quality of production.

Even though Mill was considered a liberal in his own day, in many ways his views sound to us more like those that today we associate with political conservatism. But the proof that he was not a pure "supply-side" theorist can be seen in the restrictions he placed on the <u>laisser-faire</u> doctrine. He excluded from the application of his "hands-off" policy any products that the buyer is not competent to judge or any product "in the quality of which society has much at stake." Mill said,

> There are . . . things of the worth of which the demand of the market is no test, things . . . the want of which is least felt where the need is greatest. This is peculiarly true of those things which are chiefly useful as tending to raise the character of human beings. The uncultivated cannot be competent judges of cultivation.

"The Uncultivated Cannot Be Competent Judges of Cultivation"

VII.
THE 20th CENTURY

Let us cross at last from old Europe to the New World and visit the PRAGMATISTS—a school that makes the first truly American contribution to the history of philosophy, and one that also provides a bridge between the nineteenth and twentieth centuries. The logician and semiologist CHARLES PEIRCE (1839–1914) invented the term <u>pragmatism</u> and meant it to be the name of a method whose primary goal was the clarification of thought. Perhaps pragmatism was conceived in Peirce's mind when he read the definition of "BELIEF" offered by the psychologist Alexander Bain. Belief is "that upon which a man is prepared to act," said Bain. Peirce agreed and decided that it followed from this definition that beliefs produced habits, and that the way to distinguish between beliefs was to compare the habits they produced. <u>Beliefs</u>, then, were <u>rules</u> <u>for</u> <u>action</u>, and they got their meaning from the action for which they were rules. With this definition, Peirce has bypassed the privacy and secrecy of the Cartesian mind and had provided a direct access to mental processes (because a person's belief could be established by observing that person's actions).

Providing Direct Access to the Cartesian Mind

In its inventor's hands, pragmatism was a form of radical empiricism, and some of Peirce's claims are reminiscent of Berkeley's. For example, what Berkeley said about ideas (". . . our idea of anything is our idea of its sensible effects") is not unlike what Peirce said about belief.

Peirce's essay, "How to Make our Ideas Clear," published in 1878, was generally ignored until interpreted by WILLIAM JAMES (1842–1910) some twenty-five years later. James swore allegiance to what he took to be Peircean principles and set about to promote the doctrine of pragmatism. But Peirce was so chagrined at what James was doing to pragmatism that he changed its name to "pragmaticism," which he said was "ugly enough to be safe enough from kidnappers."

Where Peirce had meant for pragmatism merely to provide a

Ugly Enough to Be Safe from Kidnappers

formula for making ordinary thought more scientific, James saw it as a philosophy capable of resolving metaphysical and religious dilemmas. Furthermore, he saw it as both a theory of meaning and a theory of truth. Let us first look at James's pragmatic theory of meaning. In *Pragmatism*, he wrote:

> Is the world one or many?—fated or free?—material or spiritual?—here are notions either of which may or may not hold good of the world; and disputes over such notions are unending. The pragmatic method in such cases is to try to interpret each notion by tracing its respective practical consequences. What difference would it practically make to anyone if this notion rather than that notion were true? If no practical difference whatever can be traced, then the alternatives mean practically the same thing, and all dispute is idle.

James concluded from this the following principle: "There can <u>be</u> no difference anywhere that doesn't <u>make</u> a difference elsewhere."

To clarify James's point, we will take three sentences, each quite different from the others, and test them for pragmatic meaning:

A. "Steel is harder than flesh."
B. "There is a Bengal tiger loose outside."
C. "God exists."

From a pragmatic point of view, the meanings of (A) and (B) are unproblematic. We know exactly what it would be like to believe them, as opposed to believing their opposites. If we believed an alternative to (A), it is clear that in many cases we would behave very differently from the way we do behave now. An what we believe about (B) will also have an immediate impact on our behavior. What about

I now believe that steel is harder than flesh.

(C)? Here we see what James himself would admit to be the subjective feature of his theory of meaning. If certain people believed that God existed, they would conceive of the world very differently from the way they would conceive of it if they believed God did not exist. However, there are other people whose conceptions of the world would be <u>practically</u> identical (i.e., identical in practice) whether they believed that God did or did not exist. For these people, the propositions "God exists" and "God does not exist" would <u>mean</u> (practically) the same thing. For certain other people who find themselves somewhere between these two extremes, the proposition "God exists" <u>means</u> something like this: "On Sunday, I put on nice clothes and go to church." That is because, for them, engaging in this activity is the only practical outcome of their belief (and a belief just is a rule for action, as Peirce had said).

I am dressed up, therefore God exists.

A Pragmatic Proof of God's Existence

So much for the pragmatic theory of meaning. Now for the pragmatic theory of truth. James had this to say about truth: ". . . ideas (which themselves are but parts of our experience) become true just insofar as they help us to get into satisfactory relation with other parts of our experience, . . . Truth in our ideas means their power to 'work.'" James also said (perhaps less felicitously) that the issue was that of the "cash value" of ideas.

If we return to our three model sentences, we will see that (A) certainly <u>works</u>. Believing that steel is harder than flesh definitely puts us in a much more satisfactory relation to the rest of our experience than does believing the opposite. For most of us, (B) usually does <u>not</u> work. Under typical conditions, believing that there is a Bengal tiger loose outside the room we now occupy would put us in a paranoid relation with the rest of our experience. Of course, <u>some</u>times believing it to be true <u>would</u> work. (Namely, we are tempted to say, when there really is a tiger outside.)

What about the third example? Obviously, the truth or falsity of the claim that God exists cannot even come up for those people for whom there is no practical difference whether they believe it or not. But for those people for whom the distinction is meaningful, the pragmatic test of truth is available. Unlike the cases of (A) and (B), there is no <u>direct</u> pragmatic test of the proposition "God exists." In fact, the empirical evidence, according to James, is equally indecisive for or against God's existence. About this and similar cases, James said, "Our passional nature not only lawfully may, but must, decide an option between propositions, whenever it is a genuine option that cannot by its nature be decided on intellectual grounds." (In saying this, James sounded very much like Kant.) James went on to say that for many, the belief in God <u>does</u> work, though he was prepared to admit that for a few it did not work. Rather, it put them in a state of paranoic fear vis-à-vis the rest of their experiences. So, for the first group, the proposition "God exists" is true, and for the second group, it is false.

For Some, a Belief in God Definitely Has Cash Value

It was this subjective side of James's theory of truth that displeased many, including Peirce. This feature of pragmatism was somewhat ameliorated by the work of JOHN DEWEY. First, one last point about James: The allusion earlier to the similarity between him and Kant is not gratuitous. Both Kant and James tried to justify on practical grounds our right to hold certain moral and religious values that could not be justified on purely intellectual grounds. Furthermore, just as Kant had seen himself as trying to mediate between the rationalists and the empiricists, so did James see himself as mediating between what he called the "tender-minded" and the "tough-minded" philosophers:

The Tender-Minded	The Tough-Minded
Rationalistic (going by "principles")	Empiricist (going by "facts")
Intellectualistic	Sensationalistic
Idealistic	Materialistic
Optimistic	Pessimistic
Religious	Irreligious
Free-willist	Fatalistic
Monistic	Pluralistic
Dogmatical	Skeptical

The trouble with these alternatives, said James, was that "you find an empirical philosophy that is not religious enough, and a religious philosophy that is not empirical enough. . . ." Obviously, James thought that his pragmatism offered a third, more satisfying alternative.

JOHN DEWEY (1859–1952) was perhaps the most influential of the pragmatists—if for no other reason than that he outlived them by so many years.

Huey, Dewey, and Louie

As I was saying...

He was actually schooled in Hegelian idealism (which in the second half of the nineteenth century had a great impact on American and British philosophy, as we will see), and it left a

permanent dent in Dewey's way of thinking, contextualizing as it did all philosophy in terms of history, society, and culture.

But under the influence of James and Charles Darwin's theory of evolution, Dewey drifted away from Hegelianism. Where Hegel found humanity progressing by resolving certain logical contradictions in the ideational sphere, Dewey

Hegel Putting a Permanent Dent in Dewey's Thought

found progress in the resolution of certain organic conflicts between individuals and their social and natural environments. From Darwin, Dewey learned that consciousness, mind, and intellect were not something different from nature, opposed to it and standing in splendid aloofness above it; rather, they were adaptations to nature, continuous with it, and like other appendages of plants, insects, and animals, functioned best when used to solve problems posed to them by the natural world.

Such an idea fit easily into the schema of the pragmatism of Peirce and James. For James, however, pragmatism had been a therapeutic tool for dealing primarily with certain religious conflicts in individual psychology. Dewey was more interested in social psychology. His basic philosophical interests were in politics, education, and morality.

Jamesian Therapy

According to Dewey, as ways of solving problems, higher organisms develop learned routines that transcend purely instinctual responses. We call these routines "habits." As the organism's environment becomes more ambiguous and the organism itself becomes more complex, its responses become more "mental." Intelligence evolves when habit fails to perform efficiently. Intelligence interrupts and delays a response to the environment when a problematic situation is recognized <u>as</u> problematic. Thought is, in fact, a "response to the doubtful as such." The function of reflective thought is to turn obscurity into clarity. Such a transformation is called "knowledge." Knowledge "marks a question answered, a difficulty disposed of, a confusion cleared up, an inconsistency reduced to coherence, a perplexity mastered." Ideas are plans for action. They are "designations of operations to be performed"; they are hypotheses. Thinking is simply "deferred action." Thoughts that do not pass into actions that rearrange experience are useless thoughts. (The same is true of philosophies.)

Ideas Are Deferred Actions

Traditional epistemologists, whether rationalist or empiricist, have erred. They believed that what was to be known was some reality preexisting the act of knowing. For them, the mind is the mirror of reality. Dewey calls this "the spectator theory of knowledge." It sought to find certainty, either in "universals" (rationalism) or in "sense data" (empiricism). But universals and sense data are not the <u>objects</u> of knowledge; rather, they are the instruments of knowledge. One of the consequences of all this is that philosophy must abandon "ultimate questions concerning Being and Knowledge in themselves, and must recognize that knowledge does not encompass the world as a whole."

Strictly speaking then, the object of knowledge is constructed by the inquiring mind. Knowledge changes the world that existed prior to its being known, but not in the Kantian sense in which it <u>distorts</u> reality ("the noumenal world"), rather in the sense that it imposes new traits on the world, for example, by clarifying that which was inherently unclear.

The definition of the world as the totality of substances (things) was abandoned with the advent of modern science, which revealed not "objects" but relationships. In abandoning that definition, science also dissolved the distinction between KNOWING and DOING. Galileo is credited by Dewey for initiating this revolution, which all but philosophers have accepted. Science allows us to escape from the tyranny of the past and allows us to exert some control over our natural and social environment. And yet, it is not only scientists who "know." Poets, farmers, teachers, statespeople, and dramatists <u>know</u>. Nevertheless, ultimately all must look to the scientists for a methodology. In fact, science is just a sophisticated form of common sense. Science, or its strategies, should play the role in the contemporary world that the Church played in the medieval world. Scientific techniques must be applied both to the development of values and of social reform.

Science Must Take Over the Role Played by the Medieval Church

For Dewey, there is no dichotomy between scientific facts and values. Values are certain kind of facts found in experience, such facts as beauty, splendor, and humor. But like the products of every other intervention into reality, they reveal themselves relative to the interests of the inquirer. But Dewey's "pragmatic instrumentalism" is <u>not</u> just a form of utilitarianism. The error of utilitarianism was to define value in terms of objects antecedently enjoyed; but for Dewey, just because something <u>has been</u> enjoyed does not make that thing <u>worthy</u> of enjoyment. Without the intervention of thought, enjoyments are not values. To call something valuable is to say that it fulfills certain conditions—namely, that it directs conduct well. There is a difference between the loved and the lovable, the blamed and the blameable, the admired and the admirable. What is needed is an active and cultivated appreciation of value. Its development is a supreme goal, whether the problem confronted is intellectual, aesthetic, or moral.

In fact, the ultimate goal of action should be "the full development of individuals as human beings." Therefore, democracy and education have the same goal. Each individual has something to contribute to the construction of social institutions, and the test of value of all institutions will be the contributions they make back to the individual in terms of creating the conditions for the all-around growth of every member of society. Such growth involves achieving certain kinds of experiences that are <u>final,</u> in that they do not provoke the search for some other experience. These are aesthetic experiences. Sometimes, according to Dewey, these experiences are so intense that they are designated as "religious."

« »

Shortly before the turn of the century, an amazing phenomenon occurred in Britain, and the ripple effect brought it to America. The British discovered Hegel! This was long after Hegelianism had been declared dead on the continent. Neo-Hegelianism found some able defenders in men like F. H. Bradley at Oxford, J. E. McTaggart at Cambridge, and

The British Discover Hegel

Josiah Royce at the University of California. But the Anglo-American national characters (if there are such things) could not have been very comfortable with Hegelian idealism, and it is not surprising that a "realist" reaction was soon provoked. (Notice that "realism" is used here in the Lockean sense of naming a <u>real</u> external world and not in the medieval sense of naming the reality of Platonic Forms.) This revolt was led by GEORGE EDWARD MOORE (1873–1958) and BERTRAND RUSSELL.

Moore had come to Cambridge to study classical literature ("the Greats," as it is known there), and part of his program involved taking philosophy classes, where, according to him, he heard the most astonishing things asserted—things to which he could attach no precise meaning. It seemed to him that the lectures were full of denials of things that every sane human knew to be true. Moore must have been an annoying undergraduate. If McTaggart asserted that space was unreal, Moore would ask if that meant that the wall next to him was <u>not</u> nearer than the library building; if McTaggart asserted that time was unreal, Moore wanted to know if that meant that the class would <u>not</u> end at noon. Russell found Moore's "naive" questions to be very exciting. In his autobiography, Russell wrote:

> Moore took the lead in rebellion, and I followed, with a sense of emancipation. Bradley argued that everything common sense believes in is mere appearance; we reverted to the opposite extreme, and thought that <u>everything</u> is real that common sense, uninfluenced by philosophy or theology, supposes real. With a sense of escaping from prison we allowed ourselves to think that grass is green, that the sun and stars would exist if no one was aware of them. . . .

**Young George Moore and Bertie Russell Discover
That the Grass Is Green**

Moore continued to defend common sense throughout his life, even though Russell would go on later to find his own reasons for doubting it. (Russell: "Science . . . has shown that none of these commonsense notions will quite serve for the explanation of the world.") Indeed, Moore came to be known as the "philosopher of common sense." Common sense became for him what sense data had been for the empiricists and reason had been for the rationalists—namely, the foundation of certainty. In one of his most famous essays, "A Defense of Common Sense," Moore listed a series of propositions that he claimed <u>to</u> <u>know</u> <u>with</u> <u>certainty</u> <u>to</u> <u>be</u> <u>true</u>, including these:

A. There exists at present a living human body, which is my body.

B. This body was much smaller when it was born than it is now.

C. Ever since it was born it has been in contact with, or not far from, the surface of the earth.

D. Ever since it was born it has been at various distances from a great number of physical objects.

E. The earth had existed many years before my body was born.

F. Many other human bodies had existed before my body was born, and many of them had already died before my birth.

This list goes on and on. It is a rather boring list, but Moore knew full well that his list was tedious. The point is that, according to him, every one of these propositions has been denied by some philosopher, somewhere, sometime. The truth usually <u>is</u> boring, and we should get suspicious when we hear dramatic metaphysical theses that deny common-

... my body was once much smaller than it is now ...

G. E. Moore Reads to His Students the List of Things He Knows for Certain

place beliefs, such as the Hegelian claims: Time and space have no objective reality; the individual is an abstraction; mathematics is only a stage in the dialectic; the Absolute is expressed, but not revealed, in the world. Moore did not necessarily want to claim that these assertions were untrue, rather that they were <u>strange</u> and that no obvious meaning could be attached to them. As Moore's student and friend John Maynard Keynes said, the question most frequently on Moore's lips was, "What <u>exactly</u> do you mean?" And, said Keynes, "If it appeared under cross-examination that you did not mean <u>exactly</u> anything, you lay under a strong suspicion of meaning nothing whatever."

The Hegelian philosophers at Cambridge and Oxford in the 1880s and 1890s had spent a lot of time inventing new philosophical terminology in order to devise novel ways of talking, because they all seemed to agree that there was something defective about our ordinary discourse concerning the world. Moore was not a bit convinced that these new ways of speaking were really necessary.

what **EXACTLY** do you mean ?

He wanted to know <u>exactly</u> what was wrong with ordinary language. Moore's commitment to our normal way of thinking and talking about the world is seen very clearly in this passage from "A Defense of Common Sense":

> I [assume] that there is some meaning which is <u>the</u> ordinary . . . meaning of such expressions as 'The earth has existed for many years past.' And this, I am afraid is an assumption which some philosophers are capable of disputing. They seem to think that the question 'Do you believe that the earth has existed for many years past?' is not a plain question, such as should be met either by a plain 'Yes' or 'No,' or by a plain 'I can't make up my mind,' but is the sort of question which can be properly met by: 'It all depends on what you mean by 'the earth' and 'exists' and 'years': If you mean so and so, and so and so, and so and so, then I do; but if you mean so and so, and so and so, and so and so, or so and so, and so and so, and so and so, or so and so, and so and so, and so and so, then I don't, or at least I think it is extremely doubtful.' It seems to me that such a view is as profoundly mistaken as any view can be.

It is very clear that, with Moore, the aim of philosophy was not that of generating grandiose metaphysical schemes, nor was it even that of arriving at the truth (much less, the Truth); rather its goal was the clarification of meaning. Moore is not the first philosopher we've seen with that conception of philosophy. Much of Peirce's work had the same thrust, and some of British empiricism did as well. (Locke had said, "It is ambition enough to be employed as an under-laborer in clearing the ground a little, and removing some of the rubbish that lies in the way of knowledge.") Even though this view was not original to Moore, in adopting it he became the forerunner of a method of philosophizing that for better or for worse, was to dominate a great part of the twentieth century. He was the initiator of what might almost be called a <u>movement</u>: one that was anti-metaphysical, purely analytical, obsessed with the problem of meaning, and far removed from the social, political, and personal problems that afflicted people of his day. Furthermore, with his concern with precise language, Moore took the first step in the direction that has since been called "the linguistic turn." We will see all these features again in Russell, the logical positivists, and in Wittgenstein.

For all his virtues, Moore seems a bit too complacent to many today. His perhaps overly satisfied attitude toward the world can be easily detected in the following passage:

> I do not think that the world or the sciences would ever have suggested to me any philosophical problems. What has suggested philosophical problems to me is things which other philosophers have said about the world and the sciences.

Moore's friend at Cambridge, BERTRAND RUSSELL (1872–1970), was born into a prominent noble family. His grandfather, Lord John Russell, was a British prime minister. Bertrand himself inherited an earldom. He was privately educated, and early demonstrated unusual mathematical skills. His temporary flirtation with Hegelianism must have gone against all his native instincts and abilities. The philosophy of McTaggart and Bradley had no use for the mathematical and scientific precision for which Russell had a natural affinity. As we saw, Moore helped Russell break away from Hegelianism's fatal attraction, and for a brief period, Moore and Russell thought alike. But Moore did not not know mathematics and was uninterested in science; so even though Moore and Russell always agreed that the main job of the philosopher was that of analysis, they soon went their separate philosophical ways.

In 1900 Russell went to the International Congress of Philosophy in Paris and met the great mathematician and logician Guiseppe Peano. Conversations with him and other mathematical luminaries set Russell on a path that led to

Hegelianism's Fatal Attraction

Reading Principia Mathematica

one of his major works, *Principia Mathematica*, written in collaboration with Alfred North Whitehead in 1910–1913, in which they tried to prove that all of arithmetic is an extension of the basic principles of logic. Probably Russell's major contribution to the history of philosophy was his demonstration of the power of symbolic logic as a tool of philosophical analysis.

A key feature of Russell's overall view was his belief in philosophy's subordination to science. Russell wrote ". . . we shall be wise to build our philosophy upon science, because the risk of error in philosophy is pretty sure to be greater than in science." The fact that Russell saw philosophy as ancillary to science, along with the fact that science was changing so rapidly during the period in which Russell wrote, partially explains why Russell's philosophy evolved so much over the many years that he developed it. His most uncharitable critics claimed that Russell made a philosophical career for himself by writing a book every year in which he refuted his book of the previous year. And indeed, it is difficult to state exactly what Russell's philosophy is, precisely because of its many transformations over the years. But there were certain common denominators that survived and unified his views despite all the changes. One constant in his thought was his view of philosophy as essentially analytical. In 1924 he wrote:

> Although . . . comprehensive construction is part of the business of philosophy, I do not believe it is the most important part. The most important part, to my mind, consists in criticizing and clarifying notions which are apt to be regarded as fundamental and accepted uncritically. As instances I might mention: mind, matter, consciousness, knowledge, experience, causality, will, time. I believe all these notions to be inexact and approximate, essentially infected with vagueness, incapable of forming part of any exact science.

Another constant in Russell's philosophy was his commitment to Occam's Razor, which, as we have seen, is a plea for theoretical simplicity, an injunction not to "multiply entities beyond necessity." Russell formulated it thus: "Wherever possible, substitute constructions out of known entities for inferences to

Lord Russell with Razor

unknown entities." He thought we should try to account for the world in terms of those features of it with which we have direct acquaintance, and we should avoid the temptation of positing the existence of anything with which we cannot be acquainted, unless we are forced to do so by undeniable facts or by a compelling logical argument.

We will let Russell's "Theory of Descriptions," which he took to be one of his major contributions to philosophy, represent his views for us: From Plato forward, philosophers had struggled with the logic of the concept of existence, and many of them, including Plato, were driven to create grandiose metaphysical schemes to accommodate the problems caused by that concept. Russell found most of these schemes to be _too_ metaphysical (i.e., too much in violation of the strictures of Occam's Razor) or to be simply too paradoxical. Let us look at three such problems dealing with the question of existence:

The Golden Mountain—Which (Unfortunately) Does Not Exist

1. I say, "The golden mountain does not exist." You ask, "What is it that does not exist?"

   I answer, "The golden mountain." By doing so, I seem to be attributing a kind of existence to the

very thing whose existence I just denied. (And what
<u>thing</u> is that?) Furthermore, if I say, "Unicorns do
not exist" and "Round squares do not exist," I
seem to be saying that golden mountains, unicorns,
and round squares are three different things, and
none of them exists!—The Platonists' solution to
this problem was to say that terms like "the
golden mountain" designate ideals that exist in a
realm of pure being, but not in the physical world.
Clearly, such a view would be too metaphysical for
Russell and would cry out for the application of
Occam's Razor.

2. Consider the sentence "Scott is the author of
   Waverly." Logicians have held that if two terms
   denote the same object, these terms could be
   interchanged without changing the meaning or
   truth of the proposition being expressed by the
   sentence. (If A = B, then [A = B] = [B = A] = [A =
   A] = [B = B].) Now, the novel *Waverly* was
   published anonymously, and many people wanted to
   know who wrote it. (King George IV was particularly
   interested to know because he wanted to find out
   who was maligning his ancestors.) The king did <u>not</u>
   want to know whether the sentence "The author of

Waverly is the author of *Waverly*" was true, nor if the sentence "Sir Walter Scott is Sir Walter Scott" was true. (Though a Platonic/Leibnizian solution to the problem would be that, indeed, <u>all</u> sentences are versions of the proposition, "Everything is everything"—"A = A." But such a metaphysical "solution" could never satisfy a Bertrand Russell.)

3. Consider this sentence: "The present king of France is bald." This assertion seems false (since there is no such person); but, according to the law of the excluded middle, the negation of any false proposition must be true, so it follows that there must be truth to the claim "The present king of France is not bald." Yet surely that sentence is false too. Must we once again accept some kind of metaphysical solution to the dilemma by consigning to an ideal realm of being the object designated by the term "the present king of France," along with the ideal characteristics "bald" and "hairy"? The Platonic logicians

The Hegelian Solution

thought so. Russell thought not. (Russell said that the Hegelians would find the solution in a synthesis: "The present king of France wears a toupee.")

So here we have three different logical problems concerning the concept of "being" or "existence." The goal of Russell's "Theory of Descriptions" was to unveil the true logical structure of propositions about existence in order to eliminate paradoxes and metaphysical obfuscations. Russell discovered a formula that he thought could perform this job:

> **There is an entity C, such that the sentence "X is Y" is true if and only if X = C.**

In this formula, C is an entity, Y is a characteristic, and X is the subject of the prediction of the characteristic Y. For example, the sentence "The golden mountain does not exist" is rendered by Russell as: "There's no entity C, such that the sentence, "X is golden and mountainous," is true if and only if X = C." In other words, the offending term, "the golden mountain" (offending because it seems to <u>denote</u> an entity—name a thing) has been transformed into a DESCRIPTION (golden and mountainous), and the real assertion of the proposition is that the description is not a description <u>of</u> anything. Notice that the notion of "existence" has been analyzed out of the term "the golden mountain.")

Concerning the second problem, the sentence "Scott is the author of *Waverly*" becomes: "There is an entity C, such that 'X wrote *Waverly*' is true if and only if X is C; moreover, C is Scott." So the characteristic "authorly" properly describes an existing entity (Scott) and does so in a way that is not merely tautological. Notice once again that the notion of existence has been analyzed out of the description "the author of *Waverly*."

Finally, the sentence "The present King of France is bald" means "There is an entity C, such that 'X is Kingly, French, and bald' is true if and only if X = C." But there <u>is</u> <u>no</u> entity to which such a description correctly applies, so the sentence is false; and so is its negation because there is also no entity that is correctly described as being "kingly, French, and hairy." So we can assert that both sentences are false without violating the law of the excluded middle.

In each of these three cases, Russell applied Occam's Razor and excised the concept of existence. Russell rather immodestly said of his solution, "This clears up two millennia of muddle-headedness about 'existence,' beginning with Plato's *Theaetetus*."

The exposition of the "Theory of Descriptions" has probably been the most technical presentation in this book, and even then, it has been greatly simplified. Much

True Being exists only in the realm of Being: Plato

Being truly exists as an actuality of a potentiality: Aristotle

True Being is Perfection, and Perfection is True Being: Anselm

There is no True Being. Being is a mere word, naming nothing: William of Occam

Being is truly a characteristic of either of two substances: Descartes

True Being is monadic: Leibniz

Being? Beats me! Truly, Hume

Being is not a predicate: Kant

Being is the Rational, and the Rational is (Bes?): Hegel

Being is the manifestation of the Will: Schopenhauer

Being does not exist; only Will to Power is: Nietzsche

Being cannot be thought: Kierkegaard

There is an entity c, such that "x is y" is true if and only if x = c.

of Russell's philosophy was highly specialized, but Russell the technical philosopher contrasted greatly with Russell the social critic and activist. He spent part of World War I in jail as a pacifist. (He was disappointed that Moore joined the war effort as a British officer; and he was even more disappointed that his student Wittgenstein returned to the continent to join the Austrian army as a private.) He was a harsh critic of the social policies of both the United States and the Soviet Union, and, after World War II, he became an active protester against nuclear weapons. (He was jailed when he was eighty-nine years old for inciting the public to civil disobedience after an illegal rally in Hyde Park to protest the presence of American atomic weapons in Britain; in his nineties, he was actively engaged in preaching against the American involvement in Vietnam.) In this respect, Russell was the very opposite of G. E. Moore, who, as we've seen, never found anything to engage his intellect and passions except things said by other philosophers. In 1960 when the journalist Ved Mehta went to Russell's home to interview him about his philosophy, Mehta was met by Russell at the door and was asked by Russell if he had not heard about The Bomb. Russell told Mehta that in the face of the implications of the nuclear crisis, there was no time to discuss philosophy.

« »

The paradigmatic case of the view that philosophy's job is that of logical analysis came from a group of European philosophers who are known as the LOGICAL POSITIVISTS. Their movement grew out of some seminars in the philosophy of science offered at the University of Vienna in the early 1920s by Professor MORITZ SCHLICK.

The original group, which called itself "the Vienna Circle," was composed mostly of scientists with a flair for philosophy and a desire to render philosophy respectable by making it scientific. Their technical inspiration came primarily from the work of Ernst Mach, Jules Poincaré, and Albert Einstein. The models for their idea of logical analysis came from *Principia Mathematica*, by Russell and Whitehead, and from *Tractatus Logico-Philosophicus*, recently published by Ludwig Wittgenstein. (Much to the great annoyance of its members, Wittgenstein stayed aloof from the Vienna Circle—we will hear a lot more about Wittgenstein shortly.)

The Vienna Circle was positively antagonistic toward most of the history of philosophy, finding only Hume's empiricism and Kant's antimetaphysical stance worthy of respect.

Besides Schlick (who was murdered in 1936 by an insane student on the steps of the University of Vienna), other names associated with the movement were OTTO NEURATH, HANS REICHENBACH, A. J. AYER, and

Wittgenstein Aloof from the Vienna Circle

RUDOLF CARNAP. By the early 1930s, their passion for scientific truth was well known, so they were not much liked by the Nazis (whose views did not fare well in the light of scientific scrutiny); nor did the members of the Circle like the Nazis much, and the advent of Hitler's regime scattered the group throughout British and American universities, where they exerted even more influence than perhaps they might have done had they remained in Austria.

At the risk of oversimplifying the platform of logical positivism (but only slightly), we can say that the main project of the Vienna Circle was the resurrection and updating of "Hume's Fork." All putative propositions would be shown to be either <u>analytic</u> (tautologies whose negation leads to self-contradiction), <u>synthetic</u> (propositions whose confirmation depends on observation and experimentation), or <u>nonsense</u>. The positivists' conclusions were therefore like Hume's in many respects. For example, Carnap wrote, "In the domain of <u>metaphysics</u>, including all philosophy of value and normative theory, logical analysis yields the negative result <u>that the alleged statements in this domain are entirely meaningless</u>." Take a look at Carnap's analysis of the function of language:

We see that language has only two duties: expression and representation. Once psychology has been correctly established as an empirical science and metaphysics correctly recognized as an art form, philosophy is seen to be nothing but logic. According to Carnap, there is nothing wrong with the poetic function of metaphysics as long as it is identified and treated as such. Carnap wrote,

> The non-theoretical character of metaphysics would not be in itself a defect; all arts have this non-theoretical character without thereby losing their high value for personal as well as social life. The danger lies in the <u>deceptive</u> character of metaphysics; it gives the illusion of knowledge without actually giving any knowledge.

Even some of Hume's skeptical musings were too metaphysical for the positivists. Hume had claimed that there was no good reason to believe that any event ever caused another event because there was no sense datum representing any <u>cause</u>, only sense data representing series of events. But for Schlick, Hume's search for an entity to correspond to the name "cause" was itself suspect. Schlick said, "The word cause, as used in everyday life, implies <u>nothing</u> but regularity of sequence because <u>nothing else</u> is used to verify the propositions in which it occurs. . . . The criterion of causality is successful prediction. That is all we can say."

Schlick's comments about causality reveal another feature of the positivistic view, namely, that (in the case of synthetic claims) <u>the meaning of a proposition is its method of verification</u>. Furthermore, the language of verification would have to be reduced to what were called "protocol sentences." Protocol sentences were to be assertions

"I saw a book."

The person whose acquaintances call him M.S., and whose passport Nº 13456 is registered with the Austrian government, and who is myself, could correctly have said on May 6th, 1934, at 3:03 PM in room 301 of the University of Vienna, "I perceive red."

Red here now

GRUNT!

that expressed the raw verifiable facts with complete simplicity. These sentences would be " the absolutely indubitable starting points of all knowledge," according to Schlick. An example would be "Moritz Schlick perceived red on the 6th of May, 1934, at 3:03 p.m. in the room numbered 301 in the Philosophy Hall at the University of Vienna." The logical positivists, looking for **incorrigibility** as the foundation of science, decided that even protocol sentences were not certain enough because they did not designate the <u>simplest</u> facts, so they tried to reduce protocol sentences yet further to what they called "confirmation sentences," an example of which would be "Red here now." These were more certain because they were less complex than protocol sentences; but the trouble with them turned out to be that the act of writing down the phrase "here now" produced a meaning not identical to the actual pointing that took place when the confirmation sentence was uttered. Not only that, but to name the experience as "red" seemed to transcend the perceptual event by categorizing it as a member of the class of red experiences, thereby referring to more than what was actually present in the experience. Ultimately, it was suggested that certainty could only be found in an act of <u>pointing</u> and <u>grunting</u>.

By now it was beginning to become obvious that something had gone very wrong and that this part of the positivist program was hopeless. The logical positivists had tried to find the foundations of science, and instead they had reverted to the cave man mentality. They fell to squabbling over this problem, and it was never resolved to anyone's satisfaction, including their own.

Logical Positivists Arguing

We have seen Carnap's demonstration that metaphysics is only an "expressive," not representative, form of language. The positivists performed a similar outrage on moral language, claiming that it was simply a disguised display of emotion, often coupled with "commands in a misleading grammatical form," according to A. J. Ayer.

So the sentence "Stealing is immoral" really means something like this:

STEALING !!!
DON'T DO IT !!

Therefore, the so-called sentence, "Stealing is immoral" is really only the expression of emotion and can be neither true nor false. It expresses what Ayer called a "pseudo-concept." Such were the moral consequences of the positivists' radical application of "Hume's Fork."

Needless to say, most philosophers were not very satisfied with this account of ethics. Furthermore, as has been indicated, logical positivism began to come undone over its failure to find the much-heralded incorrigibility in protocol sentences and confirmation sentences. (As one commentator put it, the positivists set out to sea unfurling the sails of what they took to be a watertight man o'war, only to find that it leaked badly. They began patching the leaks and discovered that the patches leaked. By the time the ship sank, they were patching patches on patches.) Logical positivism came to its final grief over another internal question: If all propositions are either analytic, synthetic, or nonsense, what is the status of the proposition "All propositions are either analytic, synthetic, or nonsense"? It too must be either analytic, synthetic, or nonsense. If it is analytic (Ayer's view), it is a mere tautology and tells us nothing about the world. Furthermore, in this case, we should be able to look up the word <u>proposition</u> in the dictionary and discover it to be defined in terms of analyticity and syntheticity. But this is not the case. If it is synthetic (Carnap's view), then we should be able to verify the proposition empirically. But this isn't possible either. So it looks as though the key principle of positivism is neither analytic nor synthetic. Ludwig Wittgenstein, whose *Tractatus Logico-Philosophicus* had been the main inspiration of positivism, took the heroic step of claiming that it was nonsense (though, as we will see, he thought <u>some</u> nonsense was better than other nonsense). This pretty much spelled the end of logical positivism. Perhaps Professor Jon Wheatley was writing its obituary when he said, "Logical positivism is one of the very few philosophical positions which can be easily shown to be dead wrong, and that is its principal claim to fame."

Some Nonsense Is Better Than Other Nonsense (After Sir John Tenniel)

There were a number of European thinkers who had continued to work well within the continental philosophical tradition despite the unrelenting attack on that tradition by the logical positivists. Primary among them was EDMUND HUSSERL (1859–1938), the founder of a philosophy that he called "phenomenology" (from the Greek phainómenon meaning "appearance"—hence, the study of appearances). He traced the roots of his view to the work of Descartes. Like Descartes, Husserl placed consciousness at the center of all philosophizing, but Husserl had learned from Kant that a theory of consciousness must be as concerned with the FORM of consciousness as with its CONTENT (Descartes had failed to realize this), so he developed a method that would demonstrate both the structure and the content of the mind. This method would be purely descriptive and not theoretical. That is, it would describe the way the world actually reveals itself to consciousness without the aid of any theoretical constructs from either philosophy or science. This method laid bare the world of what Husserl called "the natural standpoint," which is pretty much the everyday world as experienced unencumbered by the claims of philosophy and science. Writing about "the natural standpoint" in Ideas: General Introduction to Pure Phenomenology, Husserl said,

> I am aware of a world, spread out in space endlessly, and in time becoming and become, without end. I am aware of it, that means, first of all, I discover it immediately, intuitively, I experience it. Through sight, touch, hearing, etc., . . . corporeal things . . . are for me simply there, . . . "present," whether or not I pay them special attention . . . .

This "world of the natural standpoint" is the absolute

Skepti-cism		The World of Rock		The World of Chemistry		The Poultry World	
The World of Metaphysics		The World of Music		The World of Physics		The Computer World	
The World of PHILOSOPHY		The World of ART		The World of SCIENCE		The World of BUSINESS	

THE   LIVED   WORLD

Worlds upon Worlds

beginning of all philosophy and science. It is the world as actually LIVED. Other worlds can be built up upon the "LIVED WORLD" but can never replace it nor undermine it. For human beings ultimately there is only the lived world of the natural standpoint. But Husserl wanted to "get behind" the content of the natural standpoint to reveal its structure. To do so, he employed a method like Descartes's "radical doubt," a method that Husserl called "phenomenological reduction" (or <u>epochê</u>: a Greek word meaning "suspension of belief"). This method "brackets" any experience whatsoever and describes it while suspending all presuppositions and assumptions normally made about that experience. "Bracketing" the experience of looking at a coffee cup, for instance, requires suspending the

Prof. Edmund Husserl Performs an Epochê on a Coffee Cup

belief that the cup is <u>for</u> holding coffee and that its handle is <u>for</u> grasping. Bracketing reveals the way the cup presents itself to consciousness as a number of possible <u>structures</u>. (I can't see the front and the back at the same time, nor the top and the bottom, nor see more than one of its possible presentations at any given moment.)

If we apply the "epochê" to the more philosophically significant example of the experience of <u>time</u>, we must suspend all belief in clocks, train schedules, and calendars. Then we will discover that LIVED TIME is always experienced as an eternal NOW, which is tempered by a memory of earlier "nows" (the "thenness" of the past) and is always rushing into the semiexperienceable but ultimately nonexperienceable thenness of the future. Phenomenologically speaking, the time is always "Now." To do anything is to do something <u>now</u>. You can never act <u>then</u>.

Similarly, a phenomenological reduction of the experience of <u>space</u> reveals the difference between LIVED SPACE and MAPPED SPACE. Lived space is always experienced in terms of a "HERE/THERE" dichotomy, in which I am always "here," and everything else is always at different intensities of "thereness." (Jean-Paul Sartre, Husserl's errant disciple, would later draw very pessimistic conclusions from this discovery.) So the "HERE/NOW" experience is the "ground zero" of the experience of space and time. It is somehow the locus of the self.

From the Natural Standpoint

From the Standpoint of the Epoché

One of Husserl's main insights (actually derived from the work of his teacher Franz von Brentano), and one which was to be incorporated into both the later phenomenological tradition and the analytic tradition, was his treatment of the INTENTIONALITY of all consciousness (i.e., its referentiality). The Husserlian motto here is "All consciousness is consciousness of . . . ." (That means there is no such thing as self-enclosed thought; one thinks about something: You can't be just aware—you have to be aware of something, and afraid of something, and concerned about something. There are no intransitive mental states, not even Kierkegaard's "dread"—the fear of absolutely nothing. It is still the fear of nothing.) It is this "intentionality" (or referentiality) that distinguishes consciousness from everything else in the universe.

Husserl claimed that the phenomenological suspension could be performed on the <u>object</u> of intentionality (e.g., the coffee cup) or on the act of consciousness itself. Therefore, he believed it was possible to step back from normal consciousness into a kind of pure consciousness, a transcendental ego, a self-behind-the-self, which, like Descartes's "I AM" (but more deeply real), would be the starting point of all knowledge. Husserl's ideas get very complex here, and few of his disciples have chosen to follow him into these ethereal regions.

The Self Behind the Self (But Is There a Self Behind the Self Behind the Self?)

Today, Husserl is most admired for his METHOD. This method has had a number of outstanding adherents, including Martin Heidegger, Maurice Merleau-Ponty, and Jean-Paul Sartre. Shortly, we will review the philosophies of Heidegger and Sartre, Husserl's best-known, if most wayward, disciples, and we will let them represent the outcome of the evolution of phenomenology into existentialism. First, however, one last look at the analytic tradition.

« »

The author of the *Tractatus Logico-Philosophicus*, the book that so inspired the logical positivists, was LUDWIG WITTGENSTEIN (1889–1951). He has earned himself a longer discussion in this overview than have most philosophers because he has the unusual distinction of having inspired <u>two</u> philosophical movements: logical positivism and what came to be known as "ordinary language philosophy." Each of these movements dominated a large portion of the analytic

Was sich überhaupt sagen lässt, lässt sich klar sagen; und wovon man nicht reden kann, darüber muss man schweigen.

tradition in this century, and, ironically, in many respects the later movement refutes the earlier movement.

Wittgenstein was born into a wealthy, refined, Viennese family. Uninterested in material riches, he gave away his entire inheritance. In 1911 he went to Manchester, England, to study aeronautical engineering. His genius for mathematical thinking was soon recognized, and he was directed to Cambridge to study with Bertrand Russell. When Wittgenstein returned to Austria to enlist in the army during World War I, one story has it that he put a ream of paper in his backpack and went into the trenches with it. He was soon taken captive by the Italians and, as a prisoner of war, set about writing the *Tractatus* (which puts that work in the category of "great books written in jail," along with Boethius's *The Consolations of Philosophy* and part of Cervantes' *Don Quixote*).

The Tractatus, which is barely 100 pages long, is set up as a series of seven propositions. Each proposition is followed by a sequence of numbered observations about each proposition, or observations about the observations, or observations about the observations about the observations. For instance, the first page begins thus:

Proposition 1: The World Is All That Is the Case

1.   The world is all that is the case.

1.1   The world is the totality of facts, not of things.

1.11   The world is determined by the facts, and by their being <u>all</u> the facts.

1.12   For the totality of facts determines what is the case, and also whatever is not the case.

1.13   The facts in logical space are the world.

1.2   The world divides into facts.

1.21   Each item can be the case or not the case while everything else remains the same.

2.   What is the case—a fact—is the existence of states of affairs.

Wittgenstein held the view that, because we can say true things about the world, the structure of language must somehow reflect the structure of the world. That is part of what it means to say in 1.1, "The world is the totality of facts, not of things." Now, what are the facts of which the world consists? They are, to use Russell's term, "atomic facts." They are the simplest facts that can be asserted and are the simple truths into which all other more complex truths can be analyzed. In the *Tractatus*, Wittgenstein did not say exactly what these facts were, and it was these that the positivists were seeking with their attempts to construct "protocol sentences" and "confirmation sentences."

The positivists liked other features of the *Tractatus* as well. They particularly approved of the conception of philosophy which Wittgenstein put forth:

> Most of the propositions and questions to be found in philosophical works are not false but nonsensical. Consequently we cannot give any answer to questions of this kind, but can only establish that they are nonsensical (4.003).

> The correct method in philosophy would really be the following: to say nothing except what can be said, i.e., the propositions of natural science—i.e., something that has nothing to do with philosophy—and then, when ever someone else wanted to say something metaphysical, to demonstrate to him that he had failed to give a meaning to certain signs in his propositions . . . <u>this</u> method would be the only strictly correct one (6.53).

It Cannot Be Said

These paragraphs seem to express perfectly the "hard-liner" position of logical positivists. No surprise that the latter thought of Wittgenstein as one of their own. However, there were certain puzzling statements in the *Tractatus* that created quite a bit of discomfort for the members of the Vienna Circle. For example, Wittgenstein wrote, "The whole sense of this book might be summed up in the following words: what can be said at all can be said clearly and what we cannot talk about we must consign to silence." Now, the positivists wanted to interpret Wittgenstein as saying here, "Metaphysicians, shut up!" But Wittgenstein himself seemed curiously attracted to what he called "the silence" and made further enigmatic allusions to it. In proposition 6.54 he wrote,

> My propositions serve as elucidations in the following way: anyone who understands me eventually recognizes them as nonsensical, when he has used them—as steps—to climb up beyond them. (He must, so to speak, throw away the ladder after he has climbed up it.) He must transcend these propositions and then he will see the world aright.

It was here that Wittgenstein was admitting that his own propositions were nonsense, but apparently a special kind of <u>higher</u> nonsense. What would higher nonsense be like? Wittgenstein continued:

"<u>How</u> things are in the world is a matter of complete indifference for what is higher. God does not reveal himself <u>in</u> the world" (6.432).

"It is not <u>how</u> things are in the world that is mystical, but <u>that</u> it exists" (6.44).

". . . The solution to the enigma of life in space and time lies <u>outside</u> space and time" (6.4312).

Slowly and in horror the truth dawned on the Vienna Circle. Wittgenstein was a mystic! He was <u>worse</u> than the metaphysicians.

For a while, Wittgenstein seemed satisfied with the *Tractatus*. It had answered all the philosophy questions that could be sensibly asked.

As he had written: "When the answer cannot be put into words, neither can the question be put into words. The <u>riddle</u> does not exist. If a question can be framed at all, it is possible to answer it" (6.5).

Wittgenstein dropped out of philosophy. He went off into the villages of the Austrian Alps as a primary school-teacher. But he was not completely happy in his new work, and his mind was not at rest. Russell spearheaded a move to get Wittgenstein to return to Cambridge and to have the *Tractatus* accepted as Wittgenstein's doctoral dissertation. Wittgenstein was given the professional chair of the retiring G. E. Moore, and much excitement was generated over the fact that Wittgenstein had returned to philosophy.

However, word soon got around that what Wittgenstein was now saying about philosophy was not what had been expected of him. It was not easy to know exactly what <u>was</u> going on, however, because the eccentric Wittgenstein was very secretive about his new views and he insisted that his students be so too. Nevertheless, some mimeographed copies of notes from his lectures began to circulate. It was not until after his death that his work from this period was published as *Philosophical Investigations*. But long before the appearance of that book, it had become clear that a major shift had taken place in Wittgenstein's thinking.

Both the positivism and the mysticism of the *Tractatus* were gone, for better or for worse. Yet there continued to be some common denominators between the two works. Philosophy was still seen as essentially the concern with meaning, and it was still very much language-oriented. In the *Tractatus*, Wittgenstein had written, "<u>The limits of my language</u> are the limits of my world." That view continued to hold in the *Investigations*, but language itself now seemed much less limited than it had been in the earlier book.

Let us start our discussion of the *Investigations* with a look at the problem of meaning. Throughout the history of philosophy, from Plato to the *Tractatus*, the key model of meaning was that of <u>denotation</u>, that is, of <u>naming</u>. Even where philosophers like Russell and the author of the *Tractatus* had distinguished between denotation and connotation (that which is implied <u>about</u> the thing named), the former was given priority. According to Wittgenstein, the historical prioritizing of naming as the key feature of meaning had generated a certain kind of metaphysical picture that was pervasive in Western thought and that was in error. Plato thought that words had to be names of

things that existed unchanging and eternally, and because there was no such thing in the observable world, he developed his theory of the other-worldly Forms. Aristotle thought words named something unchanging <u>in</u> the world, namely, substances. In the medieval period, the nominalists also thought of words as names but thought that they named <u>nothing</u>. Their conclusion therefore was like that of the last sentence of Eco's novel *The Name of the Rose*, namely, "we have only names." The empiricists held that words named sense data and that any word not doing so was suspect. The pragmatists thought that words named

actions, and the positivists, Russell, and the early
Wittgenstein thought they named atomic facts.

The later Wittgenstein broke completely with this tradition, claiming that THE MEANING OF A WORD IS ITS
USE. He wrote,

> Think of the tools in a tool box: there is a hammer, pliers, a
> saw, a screwdriver, a rule, a glue pot, glue, nails and
> screws.—The functions of words are as diverse as the
> functions of these objects. (And in both cases there are
> similarities.) . . . It is like looking into the cabin of a loco-
> motive. We see handles all looking more or less alike.
> (Naturally, since they are supposed to be handled.) But
> one is the handle of a crank which can be moved continu-
> ously (it regulates the opening of a valve); another is the
> handle of a switch, which has only two effective positions,
> it is either off
> or on; a
> third is the
> handle of a
> brake-lever,
> the harder
> one pulls
> on it, the
> harder it
> brakes;
> a fourth,
> the handle
> of a pump:
> it has an
> effect only so
> long as it is
> moved to and fro.

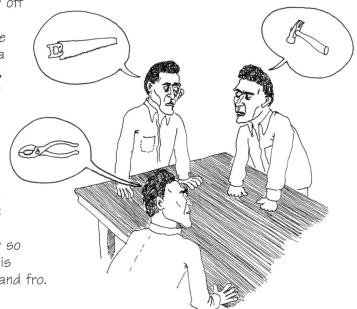

Wittgensteinians Arguing

So language, like tools or like the gadgets in the cabin
of a locomotive, can get jobs done, and its meaning is
found in the work it accomplishes. Suppose two people are

driving rapidly toward a certain destination, trying to arrive before sunset because the headlights are broken and suppose the driver says, "Well, bad luck! The sun just went down." Now, what if the passenger says, with a look of superiority, "We now know that the sun does not 'go down,' and that the illusion that it does is the result of the earth turning on its axis." Does what he said <u>mean</u> anything? No, because in that context, it gets no job done (even though in another context that same sentence <u>would</u> get a job done). In fact, there is something <u>mad</u> about inserting this scientific fact into the context described. There would also be something mad if the passenger,

Well, the sun's going down. Or the earth's coming up, as the fashionable theory has it.

From *Rosencrantz and Guildenstern Are Dead*, a play by Tom Stoppard

having found a hammer in the glove compartment, began hitting the driver with it and explained the action by saying "Hammers are for hitting." Yes, but not for hitting just anything, any time, any place. And the same is the case with language.

Still, a tool can serve a number of functions. In some contexts, a hammer can serve as a weapon or as a paperweight. How about language? Does it have only two uses, as the logical positivists suggested (an expressive function and a representative function)? Wittgenstein asked:

> But how many kinds of sentence are there? Say assertion, question, and command?—There are <u>countless</u> kinds: countless different kinds of use of what we call "symbols," "words," "sentences." And this multiplicity is not something fixed, given once for all; but new types of language, new language-games, as we may say, come into existence, and others become obsolete and get forgotten.

This brings up another feature of Wittgenstein's theory of meaning related to his claim that "the meaning is the use." He wrote, "The question 'What is a word really?' is analogous to 'what is a piece in chess?' . . . Let us say that the meaning of a piece is its role in the game." Wittgenstein generalized his claim when he called any language "a language-game." Let's consider this point. All games are rule-governed. The "meaning" of a piece (or a chip, or card, or mitt) in the game is derived from its use according to the rules. What is a pawn? A pawn is a piece that moves one square forward, except on its first move, when it may move two squares. It may take the opponent's piece laterally and is converted to a queen if it reaches the opposite side of the board. Similarly with words, phrases, and expressions—they are rule-governed, and their meaning is derived from the use to which they may be put according to the rules of the language game. There are lots of kinds of rules determining language use: grammatical rules, semantical rules, syntactical rules, and what could generally be called rules of context. Some of these are very rigid, some very flexible, and some are negotiable. This is true in comparing various games (the rules of chess are more rigid than those of ring-around-the-rosy), or even within games (rules governing the pawn's moves are rigid, but those governing the pawn's size are flexible). But even flexible rules are rules, and they can't be broken without certain consequences. When some of the rules of a given "language game" are broken in subtle ways, "language goes on holiday," as Wittgenstein said, and one result is a cer-

tain kind of philosophy (as in the case of metaphysicians), and another result is a certain kind of madness (as in the case of Alice in Wonderland). The allusion to Alice is not gratuitous. The "Alice" books were among Wittgenstein's favorites, no doubt because they are compendiums of linguistic jokes showing the lunacy that results when the function of certain features of language are misunderstood. Think of the episode when the White King tells Alice to look down the road and asks her if she sees anyone there. "I see nobody on the road," said Alice. "I only wish I had such eyes," responded the King. "To be able to see Nobody! And at that distance too!" What has gone wrong here? The joke is based on what some of Wittgenstein's followers called a "category mistake"—the miscategorization of certain linguistic facts and the drawing of absurd conclusions from the miscategorization. (According to the "ordinary language philosopher" GILBERT RYLE, this was the error made by Descartes that resulted in the mind–body problem. He had placed "minds" in a similar category with bodies, making them "thinking <u>things</u>"— ghostly, spiritual <u>beings</u> that somehow cohabitated with physical beings, but no one could figure out how.)

Or consider the case of the White Queen, who promises to pay her lady's maid "Twopence a week, and jam every other day" but then refuses to provide the jam on the grounds that it never <u>is</u> any other day. Surely this is language gone on holiday.

The Elusiveness of Jam

328

What about the positivists' search for the most simple constituents of reality on which to base the scientific
edifice? Wittgenstein asked,

> But what are the simple constituent parts of which reality
> is composed?—What are the simple constituent parts of a
> chair?—The bits of wood of which it is made? or the mole-
> cules, or the atoms?—"Simple" means: not composite. And
> here the point is: In what sense "composite"? It makes no
> sense at all to speak absolutely of the "simple parts of a
> chair."

So much for the search for "atomic facts."

In the *Tractatus*, Wittgenstein had written, "Most of
the propositions and questions of philosophy arise from
our failure to understand the logic of our language." He
still held more or less the same view in the *Investigations*,
but by then his conception of "the logic of our language"
had changed radically. It was no longer the philosopher's
job to reveal the hidden logic *behind* language, rather to
reveal the implicit logic of ordinary language (hence the
term, "ordinary language philosophy"), showing how a failure
to grasp that logic could result in "a bewitchment of our
intelligence by means of language," and to show that
unwarranted tampering with our ordinary way of thinking
and talking about the world produces a "linguistic holiday,"
which generates the jokes that comprise much of the history of philosophy. Wittgenstein said, "[My aim in philosophy is] to show the fly the way out of the fly bottle."
Apparently in Wittgenstein's native Vienna, a common fly-
trap was made by putting some honey in a vinegar bottle.
The fly, traveling on its merry way, would smell the
honey, deviate from its path into the bottle, and either
drown in the sticky, sweet stuff, or buzz to death. For

Wittgenstein, much of philosophy was like that buzzing. To "show the fly the way out of the fly bottle" was not to <u>solve</u> philosophical problems but to <u>dissolve</u> them, by showing that they were the result of deviating from the path of everyday language. This is the conservative side of Wittgenstein's thought. According to him, "Philosophy can in no way interfere with the actual use of language; it can in the end only describe it. For it cannot give it any foundation either. It leaves everything just as it is."

The apparent complacency here is reminiscent of G. E. Moore, but

The Fly in the Fly Bottle

the analogy, though good in some respects, is bad in others. Wittgenstein's mind was in constant turmoil and perplexity. There was a brooding disquietude about the man and his thought which belied the Vermeer-like bourgeois self-satisfaction of passages like the one above.

« »

MARTIN HEIDEGGER (1889–1976) was an early colleague of Husserl and a student of his phenomenology, but it soon became clear that his philosophical concerns were quite different from Husserl's. The latter's phenomenological reduction claimed to discover certain essential features of objects like coffee cups and match boxes and to provide an account of our knowledge of these kinds of beings. Heidegger, however, was interested in applying the method

Martin Heidegger

to a deeper question—that of Being itself. He was not interested in questions about the nature of individual "beings" (questions that he called "ontic" questions), rather he was concerned about the Being of beings—the fact that individual beings <u>are</u> at all (what he called "ontological" concerns). We saw that Gottfried Leibniz in the seventeenth century had asked the primary ontological question, "Why is there something rather than nothing?", but he had asked it only as a theological query in order to prove the existence of God. Furthermore, by Leibniz's time it was already too late to ask the question correctly, according to Heidegger, for Being had already been concealed in the Western tradition by 1000 philosophical and scientific misconceptions. But it had not always been so. The pre-Socratics had been astounded in the presence of Being and had asked truly ontological questions.

But these TRUE THINKERS (thinkers are better than mere philosophers, for Heidegger) were followed by Plato, who distracted thought away from Being and into an artificial idealistic world of Forms, and by Aristotle, who concentrated on "beings" and provoked a technological tradition in which Being itself would be forgotten. Heidegger wants to "call us back to a remembrance of Being"—to return us to our primordial astonishment in its presence. We must come home to Being—stand in its presence and establish a harmonic concordance with it rather than merely intellectualize it.

A Pre-Socratic Philosopher Finds the Being of His Own Thumb (And Is Duly Impressed!)

One thing that prevents us from returning home to Being is the language we employ to do it. It has become encrusted with the fragments and dust of a ruined past, and it must be cleansed and purged if it is to become a

Being Speaks

viable path to Being. Luckily (and quite conveniently, if you are German, as is Heidegger) of the modern languages, German is the closest to the truth, being less bespattered with lies, being more powerful and more spiritual than others—though ancient Greek, the language of the pre-Socratics themselves, remains the most powerful. The Greek of those first thinkers comes to us from a time when its speakers were direct witnesses to Being.

Heidegger mines this language, going into its deepest **etymologies**. For instance, he discovers that the Greek word for "being," <u>Parousia</u>, designates something that "stands firmly by itself and thus manifests and declares itself" and that the Greek word for "truth," <u>aletheia,</u>

Heidegger Mining Language

means "the unconcealed." But simply studying Greek or being able to speak German is not enough. A new beginning must be found that will be radically innovative and return us to origins at the same time. To this end, Heidegger generates a flood of technical vocabulary, to the delight of some and the annoyance of others. (There is still debate over whether Heidegger is really a pioneering genius or a self-deceived fraud—either way, or somewhere in between, there can be no doubt of his tremendous influence.)

Take a look, for example, at one of his characterizations of the meaning of the word <u>care</u>: ". . . ahead-of-itself-Being-already-in-(the-world) as Being-alongside (entities encountered within-the-world)." [TEN DASHES ALREADY!]

Humans have certain attitudes toward beings. In this respect, we are like other animals. But unlike other animals, humans also have an attitude toward Being itself. We "comport" ourselves toward it. We are unique not simply because only we can question Being, but also in that, in questioning Being, we put our own Being in question. We are the only being whose own Being is a question for itself. Therefore, our being is different. Heidegger designates that difference by saying that other beings <u>are</u>; we <u>ex-ist</u>. He has named human existence <u>Dasein</u> (being there). Unlike other beings, which are merely <u>in</u> the world, "Dasein" <u>has</u> a world. Heidegger rejects the "intellectualism" of most philosophers who have seen the world as primarily the object of human knowledge. For him, "knowing" is just one way of being-in-the-world. Furthermore, "knowing" is itself not just an intellectual act.

To "understand" something is to understand it in the context of usage, to understand it as something service-able or dangerous. Things are not just "present-at-hand"; they are not just objects for disinterested scientific inves-tigation; they are "ready-to-hand." The "there" of our "being-there" (Dasein) is filled with objects that are there for us, ready-to-hand. We have <u>care</u> or <u>concern</u> for them. This "care" (<u>Sorge</u>) is one of the main characteristics of human existence, care for the world around us, both the natural and the human world. And when we express care not just for beings but for Being itself, we are our most authentic selves as humans.

Being-within-the-world entails being-with-others. The "there" of Dasein is populated not only with objects for our use but also with the Dasein of others. Our relationship to others is neither that of presence-at-hand nor readiness-to-hand, for we must acknowledge that others make the same demands on us that we make on them. There is a danger, however, of giving in too much to their demands. We can "come not to be ourselves." We can be sucked into the third-person "theyness" of others. This is a form of inauthentic existence in which we live in the opinions and desires of the anonymous "they." It is a form of fear that produces a hollowness. "Fallenness" is Heidegger's term for succumbing to this fear. Unfortunately, "fallenness" is not just a side effect of bad choices. It is of the essence of human existence. We have "fallen" into a world of others. But it is possible to come out of inauthenticity through

Sorge: care for Being and care for beings, care for the future, for the past, and for the community. We are also rescued from inauthenticity through Angst, anxiety. We experience anxiety in the recognition of death. This is not the same as the simple fear of death. Anxiety is cognitive. It produces knowledge that we are going to die. It reveals to us that Dasein is being-toward-death. We discover the meaning of our being as

We Have Fallen into a World of Others

Dasein in the possibility of not-being Dasein, that is, in death. It is also this discovery that reveals to us our own freedom, for in the face of our imminent annihilation we must choose a life that justifies its own worth despite its necessary termination.

Human Existence Is Being-Toward-Death

Most of these ideas were developed in Heidegger's major work *Being and Time*, published in 1927. It contained two parts and ended with a series of questions that Heidegger promised to answer in a third part. But Part III was never written. One critic says that the path to Being "proved to be a dead end."

A Dead End?

After 1927, rather than returning to the unfinished section of *Being and Time*, Heidegger wrote a number of shorter works, some of which still have not been released in an English translation. These writings have provoked a great debate both among Heideggerians and his critics as to whether Heidegger changed his mind after 1927 concerning the key philosophical questions. There seems to be at least a change of emphasis, in which LANGUAGE (the new path to Being) almost eclipses Being, including

338

the human being, as language swallows up the individual. "Language is the house of Being. Man dwells in this house." It is not that humans speak language but that language speaks itself through humans. It follows therefore that poets rather than philosophers are the true custodians of Being—and particularly the German poet Freidrich Hölderlin, who conveniently happened to be from Heidegger's neck of the woods but who inconveniently ended up in an asylum. The key feature of poetry is a kind of naming, nomination, an act that "realizes" in the sense of making real. As in Nietzsche, the Platonic hierarchy has been inverted. It is the artists and not the scientists who speak Truth. Eventually, in Heidegger's final works, poetic language itself seems to give way to the poetic silence between words. Truth would have to be "silence about silence."

Despite the enormous influence of Heidegger's philosophy, a shadow has been cast over his life and his work. In 1933, as rector of the University of Freiburg, Heidegger had joined the Nazi party and had given speeches praising Adolf Hitler. Within a year, he resigned his post and issued no more praise of the Führer. In fact, Heidegger himself came under the scrutiny of the Nazis. Yet he never publicly apologized for his support of a party that was soon to commit unimaginable atrocities, and he remained silent about the holocaust. What is the connection between his silence and the Silence that speaks Truth? Apparently none. His critics say that his silence conceals a sinister truth. They also claim to find a concordance between his bombastic pseudo-intellectual German diction and his obsession with death and land, on the one hand, and the ghoulish and vacuous ideas of Nazism on the other. His defenders say that Heidegger was a politically naive philosophical genius who made a political mistake and, when he realized it was a mistake, made another by not publicly denouncing his first mistake. They say this major personal flaw does not detract from the value of his work.

《 》

Another of Edmund Husserl's erstwhile disciples was JEAN-PAUL SARTRE (1905–1980). Besides being one of the most important philosophers of the twentieth century, Sartre was also an essayist, novelist, and

Jean-Paul Sartre

playwright. His early philosophical ideas are developed in his novel *Nausea* (1938); in his treatises, *Transcendence of the Ego* (1936), *Being and Nothingness* (1943); and in his essay "Existentialism Is a Humanism" (1946). In these works, we see the influence not only of Husserl but also of Heidegger and Kierkegaard.

First, let us look at Sartre's theory of consciousness. From Husserl, Sartre had learned that consciousness is always referential, in that it always refers beyond itself to an <u>object</u>.

Consciousness always refers

Unreflected consciousness

"Unreflected consciousness" is consciousness before it is reflected upon or philosophized about. When I read a novel, the object of the unreflected consciousness is the hero of the novel.

When I run to catch a trolley, the object of the unreflected consciousness is "streetcar-to-be-caught." In unreflected consciousness, there is no self, no "I" to be

Reflective consciousness — consciousness reflecting on consciousness

found—only its objects exist, Don Quixote, or the streetcar. "Reflective consciousness" is consciousness that reflects on itself. According to Sartre (and contrary to Descartes), the "ego," or the "I," is to be discovered only in reflected consciousness. It is not only <u>discovered</u> there, but it also is actually partially created there.

Once we study consciousness phenomenologically ("bracket" it, make it the object of reflective consciousness), we discover that it is "a monstrous, impersonal spontaneity" in which thoughts come and go at <u>their</u> will, not ours. This spontaneity is a form of dizzying freedom, according to Sartre, and contemplation of it leads to anguish. We actively struggle to impose order on this free spontaneity, and when we fail, neurosis and psychosis ensue.

Sartre mentions the case of a woman who dreaded her husband's leaving for work because she feared that upon his departure she would sit nude in the window like a prostitute. Because she knew she was <u>free</u> to do so, she feared she <u>would</u> do so. (This theme was inspired by Kierkegaard's account of DREAD. When God told Adam not to eat the apple, Adam then knew that he <u>could</u> eat it— that he was <u>free</u> to do so—and he knew that if he could, he <u>might</u>. That is, he experienced his freedom as dread.)

In our own case, as in the case of that woman, sometimes the order we impose upon consciousness breaks down, and consciousness is revealed to us as the monstrous spontaneity that it is.

As a philosophical exercise, Husserl had suspended all beliefs and all "normality" in the epochê, but Sartre discovers that an epochê can break in upon us when we least expect it, not as a philosophical exercise but as a crisis of consciousness, as when we look into a chasm, and suddenly feel the urge to throw ourselves in.

This is what happens to Roquentin, the "hero" of Sartre's novel *Nausea*, as he sits on a park bench looking at the knotted roots of a chestnut tree.

Suddenly, all the old assumptions break down, and he sees the tree not as a <u>tree</u> but as a "black, knotty, raw, doughy, melted, soft, monstrous, naked, obscene, frightening lump of existence." Suddenly, the tree's BEING has presented itself to him. Roquentin discovers that Being, as it reveals itself in the crisis of consciousness, is pure superfluity, pure excess.

The rationalists, Spinoza and Leibniz, were badly mistaken. Not only is Being not necessary, but it also is ABSURD. Far from there existing a "sufficient reason" for the being of Being, there is no reason for it to exist at all. So the Sartrean existentialist finds his own existence as a superfluity in an absurd world. Yet the human being _does_ exist. He has been thrown into a meaningless world without his permission. What is the relation between the human being and the world?

The most significant form of this relationship is that of "the question." By questioning the world, I reveal a <u>nothingness</u> in Being. When I seek Pierre in a café and discover that Pierre is <u>not</u> there, I reveal a nothingness in reality. (Pierre's absence is <u>real</u>.)

In the same way, I discover that a nothingness separates me from myself. There is a nothingness between me and my past (I am <u>not</u> who I was) and between me and my future (the person I will be is <u>not</u> who I am).

This realization again makes me aware that "I await myself in the future. Anguish is the fear of not finding myself there, of no longer even wishing to be there." This anguish stems from my discovery that my "self" is not a stable, solid entity that lasts through time; rather, it is a <u>creation</u> that I must make and remake from moment to moment.

I Await Myself in the Future

Not only must I create myself, but I must also create my world. I do so by bestowing values on the world. According to the pre-Sartrean view of freedom, values preexist my freedom. I am placed between these values, and my freedom consists in my ability to choose between these

The Old View of Freedom

preexisting values. According to the Sartrean view, through freedom, I bestow value on the world by choosing aspects of it. Freedom preexists values. Life has no meaning or value except that which I give to it. Ultimately, my choice of values cannot be justified since there are no eternal (Platonic) values, no stone tablets, no Scriptures to which I can appeal to justify my choices. In the final analysis, no set of values is objectively any more valuable than any other set. This discovery leads to more anguish (of course!).

The Sartrean View of Freedom

"My freedom is anguished at being the foundation of
values while being itself without foundation."

Certainly, my freedom is not absolute. Consciousness runs up against "facticity" in existence (i.e., that which cannot be changed). If a boulder falls in my path, I cannot change the fact that it is there, nor that it is impenetrable. But I am free to interpret the meaning of its "there-

ness" for me. It may mean an obstacle to be conquered, or it may mean that my goal of reaching the mountain top is defeated, or I may interpret it as an object of aesthetic contemplation or as a scientific specimen. The interpretation of facticity Sartre calls "situation." To interpret facticity is to create a world for me to inhabit. I am always "in situation" and am always freely creating worlds. In fact, in this respect . . .

"... I am condemned to be free."

Most people create worlds in "bad faith." That is, rather than facing up to their responsibility and freedom, they flee from them by denying them, by blaming them on others, on fate, or on "the Establishment."

But there can be no blaming in good faith. We cannot blame our upbringing, our parents, our poverty (or our wealth), nor the "hard times" because we alone determine the <u>meaning</u> that these things have for us.

We are always free because there are always alternative choices—the ultimate alternative is death. If I do not shoot myself, then I have chosen whatever is the alternative to death.

A major complication in the experience of our freedom is that we must encounter other free beings. The unity that I have imposed upon my consciousness is momentarily shattered when the Other <u>looks</u> at me and transforms me into the <u>object</u> of his gaze. I can recover my own selfhood only by looking at him and transforming him into my object. (This is like Hegel's master/slave relation, except that no synthesis is possible.) "Hell," says Sartre, "is other people."

Sartre's philosophy ends with what many take to be a pessimism that reflects the plight of the human in the modern world. Sartre denies that he is a pessimist. He makes heroes of us all. The authentic human being knows that all her acts are ultimately futile in the face of death and the absurdity of existence, yet she chooses to persevere. In God-like fashion, she creates worlds upon worlds. Like Sisyphus, she pushes her boulder daily up the steep incline of existence, without excuse and without complaint. It is, after all, <u>her</u> boulder. She created it.

《 》

Beginning in the 1960s, Europe's fascination with phenomenology and existentialism gave way to an interest in a new movement called STRUCTURALISM.

Although it had a major influence on philosophy, it actually began in the social sciences and found its inspiration in the turn-of-the-century work of the Swiss linguist FERDINAND de SAUSSURE (1857–1913). In his posthumously published *Course of General Linguistics*, agreeing with his contemporaries the pragmatists and anticipating the view of the later Wittgenstein, Saussure argued that "meanings" are neither names of fixed essences (as in rationalism) nor of sensorial experiences (as in empiricism). Rather, the meaning of a linguistic phenomenon is a function of its location in an underlying linguistic STRUCTURE.

This linguistic object is not defined by some positive feature inherent to it, but rather in terms of the negative relations in which it stands to other objects in the system. (Both in terms of its sound [phonic value] and its meaning [semantic value], the word "bed" is what it is by <u>not</u> being "bad," "bid," "bod," or "bud.")

According to Saussure, a language is a system of SIGNS. A "sign" is a combination of a <u>sound</u> (or an "audio-image") and an <u>idea</u> (or "concept"). The former is called a SIGNIFIER, the latter a SIGNIFIED. (This terminological distinction is germinal for all structuralist thinkers.) A sound can only be a sign if it is related to a concept. Therefore, there must be a <u>system</u> <u>of</u> <u>conventions</u> that relates sounds to ideas. Saussure's linguistics studies this system.

SIGNIFIER (Sound)

SIGNIFIED (Concept)

SIGN

Important!

A major emphasis of Saussurian theory is on the <u>arbitrary</u> nature of the sign. That is to say, the relation between the signifier and the signified is a purely conventional one, not one based in nature. The sound "cat" <u>could</u> have denoted the idea "dog," but it just didn't turn out that way. There is no natural connection between the sound "cat" and the ideas we have of that particular feline.

There <u>are</u> exceptions—so-called onomatopoeia. But

Wau-Wau!

And I say, Ouâ-Ouâ!

even these are usually more arbitrary than they seem. Dogs in California say, "Bow-Wow"; but in France they say, "Ouâ-Ouâ"; and in Germany, "Wau-Wau"; and in Italy, "Bau-Bau."

WHAT? No Absolutes?

There is an anti-Platonic philosophical implication in all this. "The sign is arbitrary" at both ends. That is, there are no absolutes at either end. Both the signifier and the signified evolve in relation to other entities within their audio/conceptual system and in relation to other such systems. This means that there are no fixed universal concepts. In that case, the Platonic ideal of absolute knowledge is a myth.

So the signifier and the signified are both purely <u>relational</u> entities. They exist only insofar as they relate to other entities, and the relationship is mainly a <u>negative</u> one. Saussure says of signs, "Their most precise characteristic is that they are what the others are not."

As Wittgenstein was to do later, Saussure draws an analogy between LANGUAGE and CHESS. The shape of the chess piece is arbitrary. Any shape would do as long as the piece can be distinguished from other pieces with different functions. The identity of a chess piece (or of a signifier, or of a signified, or of a sign) is not dependent on some inherent essence that it has but is totally a function of differences within the system to which it belongs. As Saussure says, ". . . there are only differences, with no positive terms."

« »

At the end of his work, Saussure called for a new science, <u>the</u> <u>general</u> <u>science</u> <u>of</u> <u>signs</u>, which he named **semiology**, with linguistics as its model, even though linguistics would be only <u>part</u> of this science. In semiology, human conventions, rituals, and acts would be studied as <u>signs</u> (combinations of signifiers and signifieds). These

behavioral signs would be demonstrated to be as arbitrary as linguistic signs and would be shown to stand in the same relationship to other parts of the behavioral system as linguistic signs do to language.

It is only a slight exaggeration to say that **structuralism** is the science that Saussure called for, a science whose specific formulation is the creation of the French anthropologist CLAUDE LÉVI-STRAUSS (b. 1908).

Claude Lévi-Strauss

Most contemporary anthropology is concerned with the organization of specific societies. It tends to correspond to a form of **functionalism** in that it often explains social institutions and phenomena in terms of their utilitarian value within the culture. (E.g., any nomadic desert tribes that became dependent on swineherding would not survive. Therefore, the prohibition against eating the flesh of pigs will become institutionalized in such societies. Hence, "Jehovah's" and "Allah's" prohibition against pork.)

Lévi-Strauss rejects the functionalist interpretation of social phenomena. Many social institutions have no utility at all in and of themselves but take on meaning when related to all the other institutions within the society. Furthermore, rather than concerning himself exclusively with the organization of particular societies, he looks for UNIVERSAL characteristics of all societies. All cultures, despite their many differences, are products of the human brain. Therefore, "there must be somewhere beneath the surface features common to all."

The search for universals distinguishes Lévi-Strauss from the mainstream functionalist movement and puts him in a philosophical tradition originating with Socrates and Plato (so Plato isn't completely dead after all!), and most clearly expressed in the modern period by Kant's search for "synthetic a priori" truths. What is new in Lévi-Strauss is the claim that the human universals exist only latently at the level of STRUCTURE and not at the level of manifest fact. (Though, of course, Marx and Freud had said something similar. And indeed, Marx and Freud, as well as Saussure, have influenced structuralism deeply.) Below, when we look at Lévi-Strauss's statement of his method, we will see the impact of Saussurean linguistics on his thought because he treats cultural phenomena the way Saussure treats signifiers.

1. "Define the phenomena under study as a relation between two or more terms, real or supposed."
2. "Construct a table of possible permutations between these terms."
3. Treat the table as the structure of necessary logical connections ("a sort of periodic chart of chemical elements"), which will demonstrate that the empirical phenomenon under study "is only one possible combination among others."

Notice two things here. First, that Lévi-Strauss's is a <u>rationalistic</u> method (rationalistic because its goal is the discovery of necessary logical relations, which are in fact a priori) in which empirical phenomena themselves are "demoted and" empiricism goes by the board. Second, that there is offered here a kind of halfway house between freedom and determinism. There are choices, but they are

Periodic Chart of Possible Social Relations

Chart #72—Mother

Mother to Son	Mother to Daughter	Mother to Husband	Mother to Her Father
Mother to Her Mother	Mother to Nephew	Mother to Niece	Mother to Sister
Mother to Brother	Mother to Uncle	Mother to Aunt	Mother to Grand-mother
Mother to Grand-father	Mother to Female Cousin	Mother to Male Cousin	Mother to God-mother

severely restricted for both individuals and cultures. These choices are at the same time created and limited by the structural system of which they are a part. Lévi-Strauss says, ". . . Human societies, like individual human beings . . . never create absolutely; all they do is choose certain combinations."

In *The Savage Mind* (*La pensée sauvage*, 1962), Lévi-Strauss tries to demonstrate the essentially <u>logical</u> nature of all human thought, including that of so-called primitives. The logical foundation of all mental activity is the recognition of opposites, contrasts, and similarities. In this sense, the "savage mind" (really, "thinking in the raw") is as rational as any. Furthermore, it demonstrates an exceptional awareness of the crude sensory data of nature and an intuitive ability to detect analogous systems within the sensual vocabulary of colors, sounds, smells, and tastes.

 The *Savage Mind* tries to destroy once and for all the myth ingrained in popular prejudice and supported by Lévi-Strauss's anthropological predecessors that primitives are like children and think in some pre-adult manner. He accomplishes this with a two-edged argument. First, he demonstrates areas of typical "primitive thinking," which are far more sophisticated than our own. Second, he demonstrates examples of cultured thought, which are in fact quite "primitive."

As an example of sophisticated thought among the primitives, Lévi-Strauss tells us, concerning a tribe in the Philippines,

> . . . Ninety-three percent of the total number of native plants are recognized by the Hanunóo as culturally significant. . . . The Hanunóo classify all forms of the local avifauna into seventy-five categories. . . . They distinguish about a dozen kinds of snakes . . . sixty-odd types of fish . . . insect forms are grouped by the Hanunóo into a hundred and eight name categories, including thirteen for ants and termites.

As an example of primitive thought among the "sophisticated," one need only consider our attitude toward such cultural icons as "the bed in which George Washington slept," or perhaps toward Madonna's bra, or toward the parchment that claims to be the U.S. Constitution. (It is <u>not</u>. We would still have a constitution even if the parchment were destroyed.) Many treat these articles like primitive fetishes.

In summary, according to Lévi-Strauss, universally valid principles of human thought hold for all peoples at all times. Historical and cultural contingencies can overlay these principles with levels of abstractions and technical obfuscations, but these never replace that which they disguise. To observe this universal logic in its purest form, we should study the "unpolluted" mind of pretechnical peoples. In such a way, we will discover the unity of the human race.

« »

By the end of the 1970s, structuralism itself began to give way to a series of splinter groups that, opposed as they often were to one another, can all be designated by the term POSTSTRUCTURALISM.

This "movement" is not really an outright rejection of structuralism. It is rather a radicalization and intensification of some of its themes. Like structuralism, it found its home not only in philosophy but also in the social sciences, in **psychoanalysis,** and in literary criticism. The bridge between structuralism and post-structuralism was constructed by the French psychoanalyst JACQUES LACAN (1901–1981) as seen in his dense and often perversely obscure book Écrits. Yet Lacan claimed not to be inventing a new theory or even reinterpreting the theo-

**Jacques Lacan Reads
Sigmund Freud**

ries of Sigmund Freud, the founder of psychoanalysis, but simply <u>reading</u> Freud's text carefully (something he apparently thought others had failed to do). Undaunted by the fact that neurology had failed to produce the empirical evidence for psychoanalysis that Freud had anticipated, Lacan claimed to find its justification in linguistics. Psychoanalysis is, after all, "the talking cure." It is essentially about language. According to Lacan, "the unconscious is structured like a language." This epigram is an invitation to apply the insights of linguistics to the study of the human mind.

There is, of course, such a thing as prelinguistic experience. It gives the infant access to "THE REAL," in all its Nietzschean dis-order. The Real is experienced as pain and joy, but the child's access to language alienates it

Conscious Desire

LACK

I WANT...
(but <u>what</u>?)

from the Real. Organic need (what Freud called "instinct" [<u>Trieb</u>]) is experienced as an aboriginal LACK. As organic need is translated into language, it becomes DESIRE, and the original experience of lack is cast into the unconscious. This explains why human existence is so hopelessly insatiable. Underneath desire there is "<u>a radical lack of being</u>." But desire cannot address it directly because desire is language-bound.

Desire takes a metonymical course ("metonymy" refers to the displacement of meaning from one signifier to an-

Metonymical Reasoning

other signifier that is contiguous to the first, either in terms of meaning or of sound; e.g., "He takes too much to the bottle," or any rhyme: "cat, fat, mat"), moving from sign to tangential sign without ever being able to grasp the absolute lack that it conceals. Lacan's "desire is a metonymy" refers to this process. Desire is translated into DEMAND, but demand is not really concerned with any particular object since no particular object can replace the forever-lost object.

If one retraces the metonymical wanderings of true need (which has been caught in the nets of the signifier), one discovers that, "exhausted in its course, desire ultimately becomes its own object." Desire desires desire. This is one meaning of Lacan's infamous phrase, "Desire is the desire of the Other." Every desire is finally the desire to be desired by the Other, a desire to impose oneself upon the Other. Ultimately, then, every demand is a demand for LOVE.

What has been repressed into the unconscious are not biological instincts because these have already been translated into words. It is <u>words</u>—signifiers—that have been consigned to the unconscious. "The unconscious is composed of signifiers." In conscious language and thought, the emphasis is on the objectivity of the SIGNIFIED (i.e., the objectivity of meaning). This emphasis disguises the creativity of the SIGNIFIER (the word). It obscures and

The rigidity here → ⟨ *Signifier* / signified ⟩ ←... disguises the creative possibility here.

even denies the fact that the signifier can slide easily past its normal frontiers to reveal amazing new relations between itself and its possible signifieds. Unconscious language and thought know this truth, but the institutional strictures of conscious thought and language ("the discourse of reason"—logos) ignore this scandalous wisdom. Conscious language uses conventional signs associated with fixed meanings. It <u>must</u> do so, otherwise we wouldn't understand each other. But the unconscious is freed from the necessity of public understanding. It can <u>play</u> with the signifier without regard for its real meaning. It can produce its own private "meanings." However, there is a bridge between consciouness and the unconscious. That bridge is POETRY. Poetic language is close to a form of unconscious language. It constitutes a kind of intermediary level between conscious and unconscious discourse. (". . . like a pair of ragged claws scuttling across the floors of silent seas.")

The poet hovers somewhere between the expressly public and the intensively private. According to Lacan, the difference between the PATIENT and the POET is that the former's poetic play with the relationships among signifiers

Silence: Poet at Work   Silence: Lunatic at Work

is strictly private. The psychotic who feared birds because he knew that, in French slang, policemen on bicycles are referred to as "swallows," lives in a purely private poetic world. This is because of an incommunicable personal experience which he has suffered, an experience which can be traced in the unconscious by following the network of signifiers in which his mind is enmeshed.

What Lacan calls the IMAGINARY designates the world of the infant (and the world of some psychotics), a world in which the subject is lost in its own imagery, in its own fantasy. The "images" of the Imaginary are representations of lived experience before that experience is alienated into language. One delivers oneself from the entrapment of the Imaginary by entering into the fullness of language, which is to say, by entering into the SYMBOLIC. By naming a thing, the subject distances herself from it. When she names it, she denies that she _is_ it. Access to the Symbolic fixates the mind and rescues it

from the undifferentiated flux of the Imaginary. It mediates between self and self, between self and thing. If there were no possibility of "registering oneself in the Symbolic," there would be no possibility of individuality because individuality requires differentiation.

Lacan is ambivalent concerning the worth of the entry into the symbolic order. On the positive side, it is this

access that makes individuality possible and that has given the human its superiority over nature. On the negative side, precisely by alienating himself from nature and creating an unconscious into which he can suppress his own natural self, the individual becomes more artificial, distancing himself from the truth of his own reality and enters into a system of rigid determinism. It is in Lacan's determinism that we see him at his most pessimistic.

When one gains access to the Symbolic, one enters into a preestablished system with its own rules and structures. The self is assimilated into a network of relations in which the self is always an effect and never a cause. The subject becomes fashioned by the structure of language. The logic of the relations between signs replaces the lived experience of the Real. The individual becomes a prisoner of the autonomous order of signs. As in the later Heidegger, it is not the subject but the language that speaks.

《 》

Another important theorist in the continental poststructuralist movement (and one who has recently come to teach philosophy in southern California) is the French philosopher JACQUES DERRIDA (b. 1930). Well, . . . at least he was <u>trained</u> in philosophy, but one of the hallmarks of his view is the demotion of philosophy from the privileged status it has always claimed for itself as arbiter of Reason. Traditional philosophy, which Derrida derides as "LOGOCENTRISM," has devalued other forms of writing, especially

The Parisian Philosopher at Disneyland

poetic, metaphorical, and literary writing, as being further from the Truth than philosophical discourse. Philosophy only grudgingly uses language to express its insights into meaning and reality. Yet, according to Derrida, philosophical discourse suffers from the same vicissitudes as every other form of speech and writing, and every attempt even to say what one means by "meaning" and "reality" must necessarily self-destruct.

So Derrida willingly plays twentieth-century sophist to would-be twentieth-century Platos. His version of relativism derives from a radicalization of Saussure's linguistics. If, as Saussure had argued, every sign is what it is by not being the others, then every sign involves every other sign. Therefore, there is never any "meaning" fully present, rather all meaning is infinitely deferred. (Derrida rec-

An Excess of Meaning

ognizes that this is true of his own meaning as well—that <u>his</u> discourse is parasitical on the discourse that he criticizes—but he accepts this paradox playfully [a little <u>too</u> playfully for some of his critics].)

Every presence of meaning or of being (because "being" can only present itself in the context of "meaning") is an absence, and every absence is a presence. Derrida designates this fact of "surplus meaning" as "_différance,_" wittingly misspelling the French word _différence_, punning on the fact that the French verb différer means both "to differ" and "to defer."

In fact, punning is very much to the point here. Derrida's idea can be partially understood by thinking of how almost all words have multiple meanings.

> "Dog," for instance, according to the _Random House Dictionary_, can be correctly used to distinguish between domestic canines, on the one hand, and wolves, jackals, and foxes on the other, _or_ it can include all these animals. It can designate the _male_ canine, as opposed to the bitch, _or_ can include both. It can also refer to "any of various animals resembling a dog." It can designate "a despicable man or youth," an "ugly, boring, or crude girl or woman," or _anybody_ in general, as in "a gay dog," can refer to feet, or to "something worthless or of extremely poor quality." It's also the name of "any of various mechanical devises for gripping or holding something," or it is a sausage, or the object of ruin (to go to the dogs), or of unhappiness (a dog's life), or, as a verb, to track with hostile intent, or to put on airs, and so on and on.

If Derrida is right, the word "dog" cannot help but carry with it some, or most, of these meanings in any of its uses. Every meaning is, to use Freud's language "overdetermined" (overloaded with significance). If we say, "but the context determines the meaning," we forget that the meaning also determines the context. (The English literary critic Terry Eagleton reminds us of the sign in the London subway: "Dogs must be carried on the escalator." And if I don't own a dog, may I not use the escalator?)

Getting Caught on the Escalator Without a Dog

Because of this constant excess and slippage of meaning, every text, philosophical or otherwise, ends up defeating the first principles of its own logic, as Derrida tries to demonstrate: The key philosophical dichotomies collapse in upon themselves, for example, reality–appearance, being–nothingness, knowledge–ignorance, certainty–doubt, theism–atheism, noumenon–phenomenon, fact–value, reason–unreason, waking–dreaming,. Or, to use Derrida's language, they "deconstruct" themselves. (His method is known as **deconstruction**.) According to Derrida, the fact that all texts self-destruct is really a fact about language, hence about human thought. Yet every attempt to escape from "the prison-house of language" is an avenue leading back to it. And because, as Heidegger and Lacan had pointed out, language creates the self (and not the other way around, as was traditionally supposed), the self itself is decentered and demoted under Derrida's deconstructive gaze.

There are other important figures in the poststructuralist philosophical movement, such as Michel Foucault, Gilles Deleuze, and Félix Guattari in France, Jürgen Habermas in Germany, and Richard Rorty in America, but perhaps the interest in the relation between language and selfhood had been most doggedly pursued by certain French feminist philosophers, notably Hélène Cixous, Julia Kristeva, and Luce Irigaray. These are important, but not easy, writers to read. Understanding them requires not just a familiarity with philosophy but also with linguistics and psychoanalysis. And one must be prepared to decode dense texts that are jungles of double meaning and eccentric syntax. Yet these difficult texts are in fact examples of the kind of feminine writing their authors recommend as a way of deconstructing the Cartesian "logos," which, according to them, is part of the mechanism of the oppression of women. For that oppression is not merely to be found empirically in the day-to-day workings of society,

Deconstructing the Cartesian Logos

politics, and economics, but it is manifested in the logos of social organization itself, in the very act of producing meaning. That which is understood as "real" is a social product resultant from a "symbolic order" (to use the Lacanian phrase), and that order is "phallocentric," that is to say, constructed by men for their pleasure and advantage. If the perception of reality is to be transformed in a liberating manner, **phallocentrism** itself must be deconstructed. This negative act of deconstruction must be accompanied by a positive act of creation—Cixous and Irigaray call in various ways for the creation of a peculiarly feminine form of language and writing. Despite this common goal, there are significant divergences among these philosophers. Here we will concentrate on a summary of some of the ideas of LUCE IRIGARAY, whose background is in psycholinguistics and who is a practicing psychoanalyst, yet who presented herself for the prestigious "doctorat d'État" in philosophy because she felt that philosophy's role as "master discourse" needed to be "questioned and disturbed" precisely because of its claim to be the pursuit of Truth.

Luce Irigaray

As a psychoanalyst, Irigaray has been deeply influenced by Freud and by the Lacanian reading of Freud. But where she finds ammunition in Freudian theory for her

attempt to destabi-
lize the logos of
patriarchal discourse,
she is devastatingly
critical of Freud's own
surrender to that
same **misogynistic**
logic when it comes
to his account of
female sexuality. For
Freud, oddly, one's
sexual history turns
on an act of visual
perception. When the
little girl sees that
the naked little boy
has an organ that is

The Little Girl Sees the Naked Little Boy

missing to her, she believes that hers has been taken from
her, and she envies the boy that addition. (Penis envy.)
Because sexual difference depends on visibility and because
in women there is nothing to <u>see</u> ("rien à voir"), woman is
defined as a <u>lack</u> and is therefore outside representation.
Women are seen as incomplete and inadequate males. In
her book *Speculum of the Other Woman* (1974), Irigaray
sets out to disrupt this absurd logic. The meaning of the
word <u>speculum</u> is itself of interest. It originally meant "mirror," but it also refers to the medical instrument used by
gynecologists to examine the womb (and hence alludes to
a "spectator"). Furthermore, it is associated with the term
"speculate" and is therefore related to the philosophical
enterprise itself.

Concerning the first meaning, Descartes's philosophy (whose analysis occupies the middle of the book) shows the mind reflecting (and reflecting on) its own being—a hollow, autistic echo chamber of sameness. These narcissistic speculations of Descartes's purport to be meditations on the human condition but in fact are only meditations on the masculine (phallic) thought process—one that is incapable of representing woman as anything but the negative

Woman as the Reflection of the Cartesian Self

of its own reflection. Concerning the second meaning, the (male) gynecologist's "speculum" allows him to gaze into the nothingness that is female sexuality, yet that instrument is necessarily shaped like the vaginal passage itself. Hence, the male gaze is after all determined by the feminine. Again, male philosophers <u>speculate</u>, that is, they gaze—yet they are unable to represent that which determines their gaze, the feminine other. (A woman privileges not vision but touch, but because touch cannot be seen, it cannot be reflected in the [male] mirroring mind.)

In Irigaray's influential essay "This Sex Which Is Not One," woman is characterized as indefinable because she is "decentered" and "multiple." Like Cixous and Kristeva, Irigaray believes that an account of woman's "difference" must involve an investigation of the feminine unconscious. She does not use Lacan's phallic "symbolic realm" as her key category in this analysis, rather she employs "the Imaginary"—connected with the Freudian **pre-oedipal** relationship between mother and daughter (usually marginalized in Freudian and Lacanian theory) where she finds a "difference" that is not simply the negative mirror image of the male.

Irigaray's account of "le parler femme," or "womanspeak," shows it deriving from this pre-oedipal domain. Her first book, *The Language of Dementia* (1973) was an investigation of the relation between the demented speakers and the words they speak. This is a relationship of alienation— a passive repetition of words and phrases that speak themselves through the demented person, rather than that person being a true speaker. Yet this is very much the relation that women find themselves in vis-à-vis phallo-centric discourse, according to Irigaray. So far, woman has either needed to remain silent or to reenact the representation of herself as (literally) <u>seen</u> through men's eyes, that is to say, replicate a language that <u>erases</u> her. Irigaray seeks a form of creative language, writing, and thought that is truly woman's—one that allows woman to represent herself, one that, as one commentator describes it, would be "open, nonlinear, unfinished, fluid, exploded, fragmented, **polysemic**, attempting to 'speak the body.'" That is, one that is very much like the writing of Irigaray herself.

《 》

Quo Vadis, Philosophia?

Glossary of Philosophical Terms
employed but not defined in the text.

(An asterisk (*) indicates cross-referencing within the Glossary.)

AESTHETICS. The philosophy of art. The branch of philosophy that investigates questions such as, What makes something a work of art? Are there absolute values in art, or are aesthetic values always relative? Can there be aesthetic arguments, or are aesthetic judgments based only on preference? What is the status of art among other human intellectual and creative endeavors?

ALIENATION. A term usually associated with Hegelian or Marxian philosophy, designating the estrangement of a subject from its own essence or the rupture between a subject and its natural object.

ANTHROPOMORPHISM. The projection of human qualities onto the nonhuman world.

A POSTERIORI. A belief, proposition,* or argument is said to be a posteriori if its truth can be established only through observation. Classical empiricism* was an attempt to show that all significant knowledge about the world is based on a posteriori truths.

A PRIORI. A belief, proposition,* or argument is said to be a priori if its truth can be known independently of observation. Definitions, arithmetic, and the principles of logic are usually held to be a priori. Classical rationalism* was an attempt to show that all significant knowledge of the world is based on a priori truths, which most of the rationalists associated with innate ideas.

ARIANISM. A fourth-century heresy named after its leader Arius who denied the doctrine of the Trinity, holding that Christ had his own essence, which was divine, but which was independent of God's essence.

CARTESIAN. The adjectival form of René Descartes's name. For example, "Cartesian philosophy" is the philosophy of Descartes.

DECONSTRUCTION. The creation of the contemporary French philosopher Jacques Derrida, based on his eccentric but provocative reading of the linguistic theory of Ferdinand de Saussure. Deconstruction is a theory of texts (philosophical, fictional, legal, scientific), according to which, due to the very nature of thought and language, almost all traditional texts can be shown to "deconstruct" themselves, that is, to undermine and refute their own theses.

DEDUCTION. A form of argument in which the conclusion follows necessarily from the premises.

DETERMINISM. The view that every event that occurs, occurs necessarily. Every event follows inevitably from the events that preceded it. There is no randomness* in reality; rather, all is law-governed. Freedom* either does not exist (hard determinism), or exists in such a way as to be compatible with necessity* (soft determinism).

DEUS EX MACHINA. A phoney solution. Literally "god from a machine." Greek dramatists of inferior quality would create complex plots loaded with difficult problems, then, with the use of a machine, drop a god onto the stage (played by an actor on a cable) who solved the problems supernaturally.

DIALECTIC. In the philosophies of Hegel and Marx, the dialectic is a mechanism of change and progress, in which every possible situation exists only in relation to its own opposite. This relationship is one both of antagonism and mutual dependency, but the antagonism (a form of violence) eventually undermines the relationship and overthrows it. (However, sometimes the term <u>dialectical</u> is used only to emphasize a relationship of reciprocity between two entities or processes.)

DONATISM. A fourth-century heresy named after its founder Donatus who claimed that he had the right to reject the authority of prelates who he took to be unworthy.

DUALISM. The ontological view that reality is composed of two kinds of beings, usually (as in Descartes) minds and bodies.

EMPIRICISM. The epistemological view that true knowledge is derived primarily from sense experience (or, in "purer" strains of empiricism, exclusively from sense experience). For these philosophers, all significant knowledge is a posteriori,* and a priori* knowledge is either nonexistent, or tautological. The "classical" empiricists were the seventeenth- and eighteenth-century Britons—Locke, Berkeley, and Hume—all of whom denied the existence of innate ideas and conceived of the human mind as a "blank slate" at birth.

EPISTEMOLOGY. Theory of knowledge: answering questions such as, What is knowledge? What, if anything, can we know? What is the difference between opinion and knowledge?

ETHICS. Moral philosophy: the branch of philosophy that answers questions such as, Is there such a thing as the Good? What is "the good life"? Is there such a thing as absolute duty? Are valid moral arguments possible? Are moral judgments based only on preference?

ETYMOLOGY. The study of the origins and histories of words.

EXISTENTIALISM. A twentieth-century philosophy associated principally with Jean-Paul Sartre but also thought to encompass the work of Karl Jaspers, Martin Heidegger, Gabriel Marcel, Albert Camus, and Miguel de Unamuno, among others. More of a shared attitude than a school of thought, it can nevertheless be roughly defined by saying with Sartre that existentialists are those who believe that, in the case of humans, "existence precedes essence." This is the thesis that there is no human nature that precedes our presence in the world. All humans individually create humanity at every moment through their free acts.

FALSE CONSCIOUSNESS. A term in Marxian philosophy, originating with Friedrich Engels, designating the psychological state of mind of members of a society dominated by ideology.*

FORMS. Usually associated with the philosophies of Plato or Aristotle. For Plato (in whose philosophy the word Form is capitalized), everything that exists in the physical or conceptual world is in some way dependent upon Forms, which exist independently of the world but are the models (essences, universals, archetypes) of all reality. Forms are eternal and unchangeable and the ultimate object of all true philosophizing. For Aristotle, forms are also the essences of things, but they exist <u>in</u> things and are not independent of them. The form of an object and its function are ultimately related.

FREEDOM. Freedom exists if there are such things as free acts and free agents, that is, if some acts are performed in such a way that the authors of those acts could be held responsible for them. Some philosophers (called "libertarians") say that these acts <u>do</u> exist, that some acts are freely chosen from among genuine alternatives, and that therefore determinism* is false. ("I did X, but under exactly the same circumstances, I could have done Y instead. Therefore, X was a free act.") Other philosophers (called soft determinists) also say that free acts exist but define "free acts" not in terms of genuine alternative choices but in terms of voluntary acts. ("I wanted to do X, and I did do X, therefore X was a free act.") Still other philosophers (called hard determinists), while agreeing with the definition of <u>free</u> <u>act</u> given by libertarians, deny that any such free acts or agents exist.

FUNCTIONALISM. The view in anthropology that socially acceptable behaviors and institutions can be explained by showing that they have survival value for their society.

HEDONISM. Either the view that pleasure and pain <u>should</u> be the only motives for correct action (called "moral hedonism," defended by Epicurus and Bentham) or the view that pleasure and pain <u>are</u> the only motives for voluntary action (called "psychological hedonism," defended by Hobbes).

IDEALISM. The ontological view that, ultimately, every existing thing can be shown to be spiritual or mental (hence,a version of monism*), usually associated in Western philosophy with Berkeley and Hegel.

IDEOLOGY. A term in Marxian philosophy designating the status of cultural phenomena (such as art, religion, morality, and philosophy) as systems of propaganda supporting a specific socioeconomic system and its beneficiaries.

INCORRIGIBILITY. An empirical statement has incorrigibility if a person who believed it could not be wrong. An example might be, "I feel pain now," uttered in a case where one in fact does feel intense pain. Whether such statements actually exist is controversial, but empiricism* in its classical form (Locke) and modern form (logical positivism) put great stock in them.

INDUCTION. A form of argument in which the "premises" are empirical observations; generalizations are made from these observations. In induction, the conclusion stands in only a probabilistic relation to the observations on which it is based.

LAW OF IDENTITY. See "Principle of Identity."

LAW OF NONCONTRADICTION. See "Principle of Noncontradiction."

LAW OF THE EXCLUDED MIDDLE. See "Principle of the Excluded Middle."

LOGIC. The branch of philosophy that studies the structure of valid inference. A purely _formal_ discipline, interested in the structure of argumentation rather than in its content.

MATERIALISM. The ontological view that, in the final analysis, all phenomena can be demonstrated to be material in nature and that mental and spiritual phenomena are either nonexistent, or have no existence independent of matter (e.g., as in Democritus, Hobbes, and Marx).

METAPHYSICS. The branch of philosophy that attempts to construct a general, speculative worldview: a complete, systematic account of all reality and experience, usually involving an epistemology,* an ontology,* an ethics,* and an aesthetics.* (The adjective _metaphysical_ is often employed to stress the speculative, as opposed to the scientific, or commonsensical, features of the theory or proposition it describes.)

MISOGYNY. The hatred of women.

MONISM. The ontological view that only one entity exists (e.g., as in Spinoza) or that only one _kind_ of entity exists (e.g., as in Hobbes and Berkeley).

MORAL PHILOSOPHY. See "Ethics."

MYSTICISM. The view that reality reveals its true nature only in a superrational ecstatic vision.

NATURALISM. As employed in this text, naturalism is the ontological view that all is nature, that there are no supernatural or unnatural phenomena, and that there is no natural hierarchy of value. For example, humans are no more valuable per se than coyotes.

NECESSITY. (1) Logical necessity: There is a relation of logical necessity (or "logical entailment") between two propositions* if the assertion of one of them, together with the denial of the other, results in a contradiction. For example, there is a relation of logical necessity between the sentences "Linda is my sister" and "Linda has at least one brother" because the assertion of the one and the denial of the other would result in a contradiction. (2) Ontological necessity: There is a relation of ontological necessity between two events X and Y if the occurrence of the first event X <u>must</u> be followed by the second event Y. (Determinism* claims that every event is necessary, i.e., every event follows necessarily from the events preceding it; and indeterminism claims that <u>no</u> events are necessary.)

NIHILISM. Either the view that nothing exists or the view that nothing deserves to exist.

ONTOLOGICAL ARGUMENT. An a priori* attempt to prove God's existence by showing that, from the very concept of God, his existence can be deduced. This argument has been defended by a number of religious philosophers in the Platonic tradition. It was first formulated by St. Anselm and appears in one form or another in the work of Descartes, Spinoza, Leibniz, and Hegel. It has some able contemporary defenders, for example, Charles Hartshorne and Norman Malcolm. But it has been rejected by some notables, too, including St. Thomas, Hume, Kant, and Kierkegaard.

ONTOLOGY. Theory of being. The branch of philosophy pursuing such questions as, What is real? What is the difference between appearance and reality? What is the relation between minds and bodies? Are numbers and concepts real, or are only physical objects real?

PANTHEISM. The view that everything is divine. God's "creation" is in fact identical with God: from the Greek <u>pan</u> ("all") and <u>theos</u> ("god").

PATRIARCHY. Literally, rule by the father. Generally, any system in which political power is essentially in the hands of older males.

PHALLOCENTRISM. In the theory of psychoanalysis,* the phallus is the symbol of male sexual power. Phallocentrism is the belief that such power <u>should</u> be dominant in culture.

PHILOLOGY. The study of ancient written records, usually of "dead" languages.

PLURALISM. The ontological view that reality is composed of a plurality of beings rather than just of one kind of being (monism*) or of two kinds of beings (dualism*).

POLYSEMIC. Having many meanings.

PRE-OEDIPAL. A term in psychoanalysis* referring to the time in the child's life before the oedipal period. The oedipal period is when the child begins to develop an erotic attachment to the parent of the opposite sex and a jealous antagonism to the parent of the same sex.

PRINCIPLE OF THE EXCLUDED MIDDLE. Claimed to be one of the three basic laws of thought, this principle states that, given anything in the world, it is either A, or not-A (where A is any identity or characteristic): Either Fido is brown all over, or Fido is not brown all over; $A \vee \sim A$.

PRINCIPLE OF IDENTITY. Claimed to be one of the three basic laws of thought, this principle states that everything is identical to itself: Fido is Fido; $A = A$.

PRINCIPLE OF NONCONTRADICTION. Claimed to be one of the three basic laws of thought, this principle states that it is not the case that something both is and is not A at the same time (where A is any identity or characteristic): it is not the case that Fido is brown all over and not brown all over; $\sim(A \sim A)$.

PRISCILLIANISM. A fifth-century heresy concerning the doctrine of the Trinity—that is, the relation between God the Father, his son Jesus, and the Holy Ghost—originated by a Spanish bishop, Priscillian, attacked by St. Augustine in his book *Ad Orosium, contra Priscillianistas et Origenistas.*

PROPOSITION. As employed in this text, a proposition is whatever is asserted by a sentence. The sentences "It's raining", "Es regnet," and "Llueve" all assert the same proposition.

PSYCHOANALYSIS. The theory created by Sigmund Freud (1859–1939) concerning the causes of repressed wishes and fantasies in the unconscious mind and the relation of these unconscious motives to the conscious mind and to normal and abnormal behavior in general. Also the psychotherapy associated with that theory.

PSYCHOLOGICAL ATOMISM. The view held by Locke, Berkeley, and Hume (though not named as such by them) that all knowledge is built up from simple, discrete psychological data, such as the primitive sensorial experiences of colors, sounds, and tastes. (See also "Sense Data."*)

RANDOMNESS. If there are events that are totally uncaused and in principle unpredictable, then those events are random events. If there is randomness (i.e., if random events exist), then determinism* is false.

RATIONALISM. The epistemological view that true knowledge is derived primarily from "reason" (or exclusively from "reason," in the purer strains of rationalism). Reason is conceived as the working of the mind on material provided by the mind itself. In most versions, this material takes the form of innate ideas. Therefore, for the rationalists, a priori* knowledge is the most important kind of knowledge. In rationalistic ontologies,* the mind and the world are seen to be in conformity—the real is the rational. The classical rationalists were the seventeenth- and eighteenth-century continental philosophers, Descartes, Spinoza, and Leibniz, but the concept is broad enough to include such philosophers as Parmenides, Plato, and Hegel.

REIFICATION. The result of illegitimately concretizing that which is abstract, that which is general, or that which

389

defies concretization. From the Latin, res (thing), hence, to "thingify."

RELATIVISM. In ethics* and aesthetics,* relativism is the view that there are no absolute values; all values are relative to time, place, and culture. In epistemology,* relativism is the view that there are no absolute truths; all truths are relative to time, place, and culture.

SCHOLASTICISM. The name given to the philosophy practiced in the "schools" of the medieval universities, where all branches of philosophy, logic, and linguistics were developed and systematized according to theological schemata.

SEMIOLOGY (sometimes called SEMIOTICS). The study of the system of signs. A "sign" is an arbitrary mark or sound that has become imbued with meaning by virtue of its membership in a system of conventionality. Language is the most obvious case of such a system of signs, but behaviors and rituals can also be studied semiologically.

SENSE DATA. A sense datum is that which is perceived immediately by any one of the senses, prior to interpretation by the mind. Sense data include the perceptions of colors, sounds, tastes, odors, tactile sensations, pleasures, and pains. Classical empiricism* based itself on the supposedly epistemologically foundational nature of sense data.

SKEPTICISM (or SCEPTICISM). A denial of the possibility of knowledge. General skepticism denies the possibility of any knowledge; however, one can be skeptical about specific fields of inquiry (e.g., metaphysics*) or specific faculties (e.g., sense perception) without denying the possibility of knowledge in general.

SOLIPSISM. The view that the only true knowledge one can possess is knowledge of one's own consciousness. According to solipsism, there is no good reason to believe that anything exists other than oneself.

STRUCTURALISM. Based on the philosophical anthropology of the contemporary French theorist Claude Lévi-Strauss (but also finding followers in all the human sciences), structuralism is the view that the human mind is universal in that, everywhere and in every historical epoch, the mind is structured in such a way as to process its data in terms of certain general formulas that give meaning to those mental data.

SUBJECTIVISM. The view that there are no objective truths or values; all truths and values are relative to the subjectivity of the individual. (Subjectivism is a version of relativism.*)

SUBLIMATION. A term usually associated with Freud, but employed earlier by Schopenhauer, Marx, and Nietzsche, naming the process of refinement or of spiritualization whereby the more base and crass elements are transformed into more subtle or sublime elements, for example, the sexual or aggressive drives are transformed into art.

SUBSTANCE. In philosophy, substance has traditionally been the term naming whatever is thought to be the most basic, independent reality. Aristotle defined a substance as whatever can exist independently of other things, so that a horse or a man (Aristotle's examples) can exist independently, but the color of the horse or the size of the man cannot. The seventeenth- and eighteenth-century rationalists took the idea of substance as independent being so seriously that one of their members, Spinoza, claimed there could be only one substance in the world (i.e., only one thing), namely, God, because only God could exist independently. Under Berkeley's criticism of material substance and Hume's criticism of spiritual substance, the concept of substance was very much eroded away. It turned up again in Kant, but only as a "category" of knowledge, not as a basic reality itself.

TELEOLOGY. A teleological explanation is an explanation in terms of goals, purposes, or intentions (from the

Greek <u>telos</u> = "goal"). For example, "John closed the window because he didn't want his budgie to escape" is a teleological explanation because it explains John's behavior in terms of his intentions.

THEOLOGY. The systematic study of God and his properties, from the Greek <u>theos</u> ("God") and <u>logos</u> ("theory," or "study of").

SELECTED BIBLIOGRAPHY

Includes primary sources (some of the original works of the main philosophers discussed in this book) and secondary sources (some suggestions for further study), as well as a few personal comments concerning some of the books recommended.

Wherever possible, inexpensive paperback editions are cited.

General Histories of Western Philosophy

Copleston, Frederick, S. J. *A History of Western Philosophy*, in nine vols, now gathered in three books (New York: Doubleday, 1985). The author's biases are evident, but this is a "must" for serious research.

Jones, W. T. *A History of Western Philosophy*, 2nd ed., in 5 vols (New York: Harcourt Brace Jovanovich, 1969). Many long passages from the philosophers, clear presentation, and reasoned discussion.

Russell, Bertrand. *A History of Western Philosophy* (New York: Simon & Schuster, 1945). This eminent philosopher's biases balance out those of Copleston. Beautifully written.

The Pre-Socratic Philosophers

Primary Sources

Barnes, Jonathan. *Early Greek Philosophy* (New York: Penguin Books, 1987). Pertinent selections with commentary.

Nahm, Milton, ed. *Selections from Early Greek Philosophy* (New York: Appleton-Century-Crofts, 1964).

Secondary Sources

Ring, Merrill. *Beginning with the Pre-Socratics* (Mountain View, CA: Mayfield, 1987). A short, well-written account, includes most of the pertinent early fragments.

The Athenian Period

Primary Sources

Aristotle. *Introduction to Aristotle*, edited by Richard McKeon (New York: Modern Library, 1992), Contains all of Aristotle's main works.

Plato. *Great Dialogues of Plato*, translated by W. H. D. Rouse and edited by E. H. Warmington and P. G. Rouse (New York: New American Library, 1956). Contains *The Republic*, "Apology," "Crito," "Meno," and "The Symposium," among others. This is only one of many inexpensive paperback editions now available.

Plato. *The Republic of Plato*, translated by Allan Bloom (New York: Basic Books, 1968). Perhaps the most accurate and literal translation (but therefore not the most readable).

Secondary Sources

Adler, Mortimer J. *Aristotle for Everybody* (New York: Bantam Books, 1985). A readable, enticing defense of Aristotle's views by a real Aristotelian.

Barnes, Jonathan. *Aristotle* (New York: Oxford University

Press ["Past Masters" series], 1982). Almost all the books in this series are good, cheap, short, and readable.

Barrett, Harold. *The Sophists* (Novato, CA: Chandler and Sharp, 1987). A short, spirited defense of the views of the sophists.

Murdoch, Iris. *The Fire and the Sun: Why Plato Banished the Artists* (New York: Oxford University Press, 1978). The author is both a foremost novelist and a top-rate philosopher.

Pirsig, Robert. *Zen and the Art of Motorcycle Maintenance* (New York: Bantam Books, 1982). A (mostly) fascinating contemporary personal investigation of the problem of value that obsessed the sophists, Socrates, and Plato. Pirsig sides with the sophists and repairs his Harley.

Stone, I. F. *The Trial of Socrates* (New York: Doubleday [Anchor Books], 1989). Wonderful depiction of Athenian political life at the time of Socrates. Annoyingly simplistic criticism of Socratic and Platonic philosophy.

Vlastos, Gregory, ed. *The Philosophy of Socrates: A Collection of Critical Essays* (Garden City, NY: Doubleday, 1971). A fine sampling of scholarly work about Socrates.

The Hellenistic Period

Primary Sources

Epicurus. *Epicurus: The Extant Remains*, translated by C. Bailey (Oxford, Eng.: Clarenden Press, 1926).

Hadas, Moses, ed. *Essential Works of Stoicism* (New York: Bantam Books, 1961). Contains Marcus Aurelius's "To Himself," Epictetus' "The Manual," and Seneca's "On Tranquility."

Plotinus. *The Six Enneads*, translated by S. MacKenna and B. S. Page (Chicago: Encyclopedia Britannica, 1952).

Medieval Philosophy

Primary Sources

Hyman, Arthur, and James T. Walsh, eds., *Philosophy in the Middle Ages: The Christian, Islamic and Jewish Traditions* (Indianapolis: Hackett, 1974). Excellent samplings of the work of the main medieval philosophers, including selections from Augustine, Erigena, Anselm, and Thomas Aquinas.

Secondary Sources

Eco, Umberto. *The Name of the Rose*, translated by William Weaver (New York: Warner Books, 1984). A best-selling philosophical novel by a medieval scholar. (You get a mean murder mystery as well.)

Gilson, Etienne. *History of Christian Philosophy in the Middle Ages* (New York: Random House, 1955). By one of the great students of the medieval mind.

The Seventeenth and Eighteenth Centuries

Primary Sources

Berkeley, George. *Philosophical Works* (London: Dent & Sons [Everyman's Library], 1992). See especially *Three Dialogues Between Hylas and Philonous*. Very readable.

Descartes, René. *Discourse on Method and Meditations*, translated by L. J. Lafleur (Indianapolis: Bobbs-Merrill [The library of Liberal Arts], 1960).

Descartes, René. *A Guided Tour of René Descartes' Meditations on First Philosophy*, edited by Christropher Biffle and translated by Ronald Rubin (Mountain View, CA: Mayfield, 1989). Annotated with questions in the margins for students.

Descartes, R., B. Spinoza, G. Leibniz. *The Rationalists* (New York: Doubleday [Anchor Books], 1960). An excellent anthology selected from the key works of these philosophers.

Hobbes, Thomas. *Leviathan* (New York: Penguin Books, 1982).

Hume, David. *A Treatise of Human Nature* (New York: Penguin Classics, 1984).

Kant, Immanuel. *Prolegomena to Any Future Metaphysics* (Indianapolis: Bobbs-Merrill [The library of Liberal Arts], 1950). Difficult but much more accessible than *The Critique of Pure Reason.*

Kant, Immanuel. *Groundwork of the Metaphysic of Morals,* translated by H. J. Patons (New York: Harper Torchbooks, 1964).

Kant, Immanuel. *Critique of Pure Reason,* translated by J. M. D. Meiklejohn (London: Dent [Everyman's Library], 1991).

Leibniz, Gottfried W. *Philosophical Writings,* edited by G. H. R. Parkinson (London: Dent, [Everyman's Library], 1990). See especially "Discourse on Metaphysics" and "Monadology."

Locke, John. *Two Treatises of Government* (New York: New American Library, 1965).

Locke, John. *An Essay Concerning Human Understanding* (London: Dent [Everyman's Library], 1991).

Locke, J., G. Berkeley, D. Hume. *The Empiricists* (New York: Doubleday [Anchor Books], 1961). The companion to *The Rationalists.*

de Spinoza, Benedict. *On the Improvement of the Understanding, The Ethics, and Correspondence,* translated by R. H. M. Elwes (New York: Dover Books, 1955). See especially *The Ethics.* ("Benedict" is the latinized version of "Baruch," his real name.)

Secondary Sources

Ayer, A. J. *Hume* (New York: Hill & Wang ["Past Masters" series], 1980).

Hampshire, Stuart. *Spinoza: An Introduction to his Philosophical Thought* (New York: Penguin Books, 1992). Very readable; written by an excellent philosopher.

Martin, C. B., and D. M. Armstrong, eds. *Locke and*

Berkeley: A Collection of Critical Essays (Garden City, NY: Doubleday [Anchor Books], 1968). A good selection of scholarly studies.

Scruton, Roger. *Kant* (New York: Oxford University Press ["Past Masters" series], 1989).

Warnock, G. J. *Berkeley* (Baltimore: Penguin Books, 1953). Still one of my favorites.

The Nineteenth Century

Primary Sources

Hegel, G. W. F. *The Phenomenology of Mind*, translated by J. B. Baillie (New York: Harper & Row [Torchbooks], 1967). Will look impressive on your shelf, but not recommended for the casual reader.

Kierkegaard, Søren. *Fear and Trembling*, translated by Alastair Hannay (New York: Penguin Books, 1985). A fascinating little book.

Marx, Karl, and Friedrich Engels. *Marx and Engels : Basic Writings on Politics and Philosophy*, edited by Lewis S. Feuer, (Garden City, NY: Doubleday [Anchor Books], 1989).

Mill, J. S. *On Liberty and Utilitarianism* (New York: Bantam Books, 1993).

Nietzsche, Friedrich. *Basic Writings of Nietzsche*, translated and edited by Walter Kaufmann (New York: Modern Library, 1968). See especially *The Birth of Tragedy*, *Beyond Good and Evil*, and *On the Genealogy of Morals*.

Nietzsche, Friedrich. *Thus Spoke Zarathustra*, translated by R. J. Hollingdale (New York: Penguin Books, 1969). The students' favorite.

Schopenhauer, Arthur. *The World as Will and Idea*, translated by R. B. Haldane and J. Kemp (Garden City, NY: Doubleday [Dolphin Books], 1961). Big and imposing but surprisingly readable.

Secondary Sources

Barrett, William. *Irrational Man* (New York: Doubleday [Anchor Books], 1990). Classical work on existentialism. See chapters on Kierkegaard and Nietzsche. Also good for twentieth-century figures.

Fromm, Erich. *Marx's Concept of Man* (New York: Frederich Ungar, 1969). Contains philosophical essays by the early Marx and a long essay by Fromm. Both very good.

Mooney, Edward. *Knights of Faith and Resignation: Reading Kierkegaard's "Fear and Trembling"* (Albany: State University of New York Press, 1991). A fine little book by a friend of mine. Buy it; he can use the money.

Rius. *Marx for Beginners* (New York: Pantheon, 1979). Cartoons and text by Mexico's leading political cartoonist.

Safranski, Rudiger. *Schopenhauer and the Wild Years of Philosophy* (Cambridge, MA: Harvard University Press, 1990). A good way to break into the strange world of nineteenth-century German philosophy.

Singer, Peter. *Marx* (Oxford, Eng.: Oxford University Press ["Past Masters" series], 1983).

Westphal, Merold. *History and Truth in Hegel's "Phenomenology"* (Atlantic Highlands, NJ: Humanities Press, 1990). You'll need a guide to Hegel's work. This one's good.

The Twentieth Century

Primary Sources

Ayer, A. J. *Language, Truth and Logic* (New York: Dover Publications, n.d.). This short book is the student's best approach to logical positivism. Be careful Sir Alfred doesn't convert you!

Derrida, Jacques. *Of Grammatology*, translated by Gayatri Chakravorty Spivak (Baltimore: The Johns Hopkins University Press, 1976). Not easy!

Dewey, John. *The Quest for Certainty* (New York: Putnam [Capricorn Books], 1960).

Heidegger, Martin. *Being and Time*, translated by John Macquarrie and Edward Robinson (New York: Harper & Row, 1962).

Husserl, Edmund. *Ideas: General Introduction to Pure Phenomenology*, translated by W. R. Boyce Gibson (New York: Collier, 1962).

Irigaray, Luce. *Speculum of the Other Woman*, translated by Gillian C. Gill (New York: Norton, 1977).

James, William. *Pragmatism* (Cleveland: Meridian Books, 1961).

Lacan, Jacques. *Écrits: A Selection*, translated by Alan Sheridan (New York: Norton, 1977). Ouch!

Lévi-Strauss, Claude. *The Savage Mind* (Chicago: University of Chicago Press, 1968).

Lévi-Strauss, Claude. *Triste Tropiques: An Anthropological Study of Primitive Studies in Brazil* (New York: Atheneum, 1964).

Moore, G. E. *Philosophical Papers* (New York: Collier, 1962). See especially "A Defense of Common Sense."

Russell, Bertrand. *The Problems of Philosophy* (New York: Oxford University Press, 1967).

Sartre, Jean-Paul. *The Philosophy of Jean-Paul Sartre*, Robert Denoon Cumming, ed. (New York: Random House [Vintage Books], 1972).

Sartre, Jean-Paul. *Existentialism and Human Emotions* (New York: Citadel Press, 1990). Start here.

Wittgenstein, Ludwig. *Philosophical Investigations*, 3rd ed., translated by G. E. M. Anscombe (New York: Macmillan, 1968).

Secondary Sources

Archard, David. *Consciousness and the Unconscious* (La Salle, IL: Open Court, 1984). This comes as close to an "easy access" to Lacan as I've found.

Castaneda, Carlos. *Journey to Ixtlán* (New York: Pocket Book, 1975). An unusual introduction to the idea of phenomenology. Somewhere between anthropology, philosophy, and fantasy.

Danto, Arthur C. *Jean-Paul Sartre* (New York: Viking Press ["Modern Masters" series], 1975). Great!

Dreyfus, Hubert. *Being-in-the-World: A Commentary on Heidegger's "Being and Time, Division I"* (Cambridge, MA: MIT Press, 1991). The best guide to *Being and Time*.

Duffy, Bruce. *The World as I Found It* (New York: Ticknor and Fields, 1988). A good novel about G. E. Moore, Bertrand Russell, and Ludwig Wittgenstein.

Leach, Edmund. *Claude Lévi-Strauss* (Chicago: University of Chicago Press, 1989).

Moi, Toril. *Sexual/Textual Politics: Feminist Literary Theory* (New York: Methuen, 1986). Good chapters on Cixous, Irigaray, and Kristeva.

Monk, Ray. *Ludwig Wittgenstein: The Duty of Genius* (New York: Penguin Books, 1990). An excellent biography with philosophical summaries.

Norris, Christopher. *Derrida* (Cambridge, MA: Harvard University Press, 1987).

Passmore, John. *Recent Philosophers* (La Salle, IL: Open Court, 1985). Good, clear account bringing us up to date on recent trends.

Pears, David. *Wittgenstein* (Cambridge, MA: Harvard University Press ["Modern Masters" series], 1971).

INDEX

Averröes, 110, 125
Ayer, Sir Alfred Jules, 305, 309, 311, 397, 399

Bacon, Roger, 123
Bad faith, 352
Bain, Alexander, 276
Barnes, Jonathan, 394
Barrett, Harold, 395
Barrett, William, 399
Beatific vision, 121
Beauty, 49, 61, 66, 121, 243, 287, 319
Becoming, 210, 211, 214
Beethoven, Ludwig van, 227
Being, 25, 26, 58, 62, 103, 104, 109, 208, 209, 210, 211, 214, 231, 243, 262, 266, 286, 300, 301, 302, 303, 328, 331, 332, 333, 335, 336, 337, 338, 339, 341, 344, 345, 346, 365, 371, 373, 383, 387, 401
Belief, 57, 58–59, 200, 204, 218, 267, 276, 277, 279, 280, 313
Bentham, Jeremy, 267–271, 272, 273, 385
Berkeley, George, 174–179, 186, 205, 227, 383, 385, 386, 389, 391, 396, 397
Big Bang, The, 23
Boethius, 101, 111, 318
Bourgeoisie, The, 252, 255, 330
Bracketing, 313–314, 342. See also Epoché
Bradley, Francis Herbert, 288, 290, 296
Brahe, Tycho, 123
Brentano, Franz von, 315
Brutus, 162
Buddha, 224, 227
Buridan, John, 123

Caesar, Julius, 160, 161, 162, 233
Calculus of Felicity, The, 269–271, 272
Callicles, 42–43, 268

Camus, Albert, 384
Capitalism, 248, 252, 253
Care, 335, 336, 337
Carnap, Rudolf, 306, 307, 309, 311
Castaneda, Carlos, 401
Categorical imperative, The, 200–203
Categories of the understanding, 195–196, 218, 221
Category mistake, 328
Catholicism, 131, 138
Causality, 34, 68, 72, 73, 99, 119, 120, 121, 167, 186–188, 190, 195, 196, 198, 199, 267, 298, 307, 370, 389
Certainty, 91, 134, 137, 138, 139, 140, 141, 189, 270, 291, 309
Cervantes, Saavedra, Miguel de, 318
Chancellor, John, 58
Charles the Bald, 102
Christianity, 73, 89, 90, 91, 93, 94, 95, 96, 102, 104, 107, 116, 153, 155, 200, 262
Christina of Sweden, 146
Cixous, Hélène, 375, 376, 379, 401
Common sense, 15, 164, 186, 193, 195, 197, 199, 287, 290–291, 293, 386
Communism, 65, 248, 255
Complex ideas, 166
Concepts, 57, 59, 61, 92, 117, 196, 198, 231, 310, 355, 356, 357, 384, 387
Conceptualism, 118
Confirmation sentences, 308, 310, 319
Conjecture, 57, 58, 59, 66
Connotation, 323
Consciousness, 141, 163, 164, 250, 253, 284, 298, 312, 314, 315, 316, 341–342, 343, 344, 350, 390, 400
Consequentialism, 268
Constantine, 94
Constitution, The American, 173, 363
Copernicus, Nikolaus, 123